Anonymous

Newport villa owners' summer visitors' and residents' guide

to the reliable business interests of the city

Anonymous

Newport villa owners' summer visitors' and residents' guide to the reliable business interests of the city

ISBN/EAN: 9783337713232

Printed in Europe, USA, Canada, Australia, Japan

Cover: Foto ©ninafisch / pixelio.de

More available books at **www.hansebooks.com**

NEWPORT

VILLA OWNERS'

Summer Visitors' and Residents'

GUIDE

TO THE RELIABLE BUSINESS INTERESTS OF THE CITY,

FOR 1883.

Together with a List of all the Cottage Rentals, and Villa Owners who will occupy their residences during the Summer of 1883, compiled to date, and other miscellaneous information.

PUBLISHED BY
W. G. MORRISON & CO.,
WASHINGTON STREET,
BOSTON.

39 WEST THIRTY-FIRST ST.,
OPP. GRAND HOTEL,
NEW YORK.

ROB'T BAGG & SON,

TAILORS,

Uniforms
AND
Liveries.

Ladies' Jackets
AND
Riding Habits.

Ladies' Department.

Messrs. Rob't Bagg & Son take the liberty of informing you that they have opened a Ladies' Department for the making of

CLOTH SUITS.

HERE business houses of equal responsibility each offer productions said to be the best of their respective kinds, the choice must necessarily rest with the purchaser. Having introduced the Bicycle into this country, however, we shall not willingly relinquish the reputation which our six years of successful business has brought us. If you are wise enough to purchase a Bicycle or Tricycle, be wise enough also to be content with nothing less than the very best that money can procure. You may feel assured that it will prove the truest economy in the end. Find out all you can about bicycles before you make your choice, and if you will send us a three-cent stamp, we will aid you in your search for information, by sending you our large illustrated catalogue by return mail.

The Cunningham Company,

THE PIONEER BICYCLE HOUSE OF AMERICA,

(ESTABLISHED 1877.)

Importing Manufacturers of Bicycles and Tricycles,

Odd Fellows' Hall, Boston, Mass.

A CLUB ROAD RACE

"HARVARD WINS"! "RAH - RAH"!!! "HURRAH" No. "YALE" "RAH"!!

❋PREFACE.❋

IN response to many urgent appeals from a number of the most reliable firms doing business in Newport, the undersigned have compiled this volume of valuable Miscellaneous Information for the use of the Villa Owners and vast number of Pleasure Seekers who visit their "City by the Sea" annually. It being the first edition of the work ever issued, and late in the season when undertaken, a number of items have been omitted, both in the information and presswork, that would otherwise have added to its value and attractiveness. However, in placing it before the public, we trust it will be found a useful and reliable guide, thereby fulfilling the requirements for which it is issued.

W. G. MORRISON & CO.,
Publishers.

BOSTON, JUNE 25th, 1883

6   NEWPORT VILLA OWNERS'

LINDO BROTHERS,

Diamonds, Fine Watches, Rich Jewelry,

Cor. 29th Street.   **1205 BROADWAY.**   Opp. Gilsey House.

H. A. BROCK,

—:- Wholesale aad Retail Dealer in —:—

Fine Imported and Domestic Cigars.

Gentlemen Ordering Cigars by the Box will please state Size, Color and Price.

Cigars not satisfactory can be returned at my expense.

H. A. BROCK,

19 WATER STREET AND 22 SPRING LANE,

BOSTON.

SIMPSON'S

HOME MADE CANDIES,

FRESH HOURLY.

No. 331 SIXTH AVENUE,

BRANCH, BELLEVUE AVE., NEWPORT, R.I.

NEW YORK.

☀ Table �) of ☜ Contents. ☀

Newport, "The City by the Sea"

Washed by foaming waves,
On beach of crystal sand;
An earthly paradise,
The haven of our land.

As gold marks the standard of a nation's money, so does Newport hold the pivot of American watering-places. The name of Newport has become a generic term, with an unnumbered radiating family. Every State has its Newport. From the rough Atlantic to the placid Pacific, from the rocky coasts of Maine to the sandy shores of Florida, one finds an hundred children of the mother-town. The Newport of the West, the Newport of the South, and the Newport of the mountains, all translated mean a summer resort with alleged attractions reckoned from the pinnacle which is given by the " City by the Sea." But there is but one Newport. Nature made but one; the mould broke; and to-day she stands alone, protected in her exclusiveness.

Shall I tell you the history of this grand old town? Shall I tell you how William Coddington purchased the whole township of the Narragansett Indians, not with the " dollars of our daddies," but with old coats, hoes, rakes, scrap-iron and other junk-shop commodities? Shall I claim for the old place a commercial importance which years ago outranked the metropolis, or shall I give the suppositions which have supposed that the Norsemen landed upon its shores, and perhaps took a solitary dive into the then not fashionable breakers? Need I tell of its romantic career up the line of evolution to the proudest of summer cities? All this would be unnecessary, for the A B C of history has told you of its early conquests, and the World of fashion has for a score of years sang its praises. In its reputative sense Newport is a Summer City, not of transients, but of long-stay people. In the rank and file of its past and present half-year citizens stand the names which have been and are being engraved on the stones of history. Intelligence, art, music, wealth and beauty meet upon its soil in happy combination.

The wealth of the Empire State can be seen on a pleasant afternoon riding over the beautiful avenues, strolling on the beach, or frolicking in the surf. Wall Street and Fifth Avenue, Fair Harvard and stately Yale, blue-blooded Boston, army and navy, foreign ministers, ambassadors, princes and princesses, make this beautiful city the play-ground of the upper realms of society. Newport is the underspring of summer fashion, the inside wheel which regulates the ifs and buts of society life. To be a Newport belle is a proud position for fair

women. Out of the foaming billows many an American princess has found her life's partner and has pledged herself to go with the wave to the land of its next breaking.

The "Baby-state" has a Newport, or rather Newport has "Little Rhody."

I am in Newport again this summer, to listen to the dear old ocean, stroll along the shady roads, realize the wealth and admire the beauty,—alas, from afar! for I am a journalist, proud but poor, and my editorial rap will probably be unintelligible on the golden doors of wealth. But the ocean and the flowers are mine, and the water sparkles and breaks on the crystal sand for me as for the one of millions.

I am a bicycler, and enjoying this season the ripest fruits of recreation. Every pleasant day I mount my graceful "Expert Columbia" and run over the shady roads, feeling the Monarch of Wheels, and forcing Nature to spread out her nooks and corners in endless panorama. Grand old Newport is doubly graceful to a rider of the Modern Pegasus. I rise at early morning, when a new earth seems glittering in the jewelled dew; the birds are singing, and the murmur of the Atlantic adds a full organ to the swelling chorus. A glorious wheel! I

> Go forth upon my wheeled horse and list
> To Nature's teachings.

A ride on Bellevue Avenue, the one great artery of summer wealth, the most celebrated of streets,—a conservative, truly aristocratic close corporation of residences, whose holders' tenacity has held this avenue against all speculation has kept it for themselves and their posterity. I wheel by the "Old Stone Mill" on Touro Park. The key which unlocks the mysterious history of this ancient landmark was probably lost over Purgatory Cliffs. Whether the hand of Norseman or Anglo-Saxon mixed the lime and mortar which hold the rough stones together; whether it was the scene of lovers' leaps, or the looming tower of forgotten tragedies,—only far-fetched legends can shed a glimmer of light on this pile of unhistorized stone. A few turns of the wheel and I am close to the Channing Memorial Church. I admire the beautiful architecture and the wonderful stained-glass windows, a marvel of crystal-colored handiwork. Among all the glitter and wealth of Newport it is pleasant to find that the House of God stands out in holy magnificence. I wheel away; the rising sun throws its rays obliquely on my whirling wheel, and the nickeled spokes flash the sparkling light of a grand good morning.

On every side stand the summer homes of wealth. Here a stately pile of stone, there a picturesque cottage, both surrounded by well-kept lawns, shady nooks, and opening flowers. Every place stands by itself, original in plan, and rightly claiming its identity. In a few hours these little Edens will be filled with happy parties, and the now quiet avenue will be the arena of dashing teams, a merry rushing stream of life on wheels. But Bellevue Avenue does not contain all the magnificent residences. From the avenue lead many streets, lesser arteries it is true, yet claiming a goodly number of beautiful estates. One can ride for miles and yet see new architectural designs and fresh ideas of summer gardening. Newport is one vast garden, almost surrounded by the ocean, warmed by the generous sun, yet cooled by an ever-fanning breeze.

Ah, Newport is a glorious town, a perfect storehouse of grand good times! One can find a hundred places all vieing with each other in beauty and interest. A wheel over Ocean Avenue—land on one side, water on the other; rocks and breakers, hotels and bathing-houses, shade and sunshine, old houses and palaces; an "old curiosity shop" of relics and modern conveniences. I pass the Spouting Rock, famous for non-spouting except when the wild winds urge the Atlantic into a foamy fury. Now comes a long, picturesque stretch of rocky scenery, a black frontispiece fringed with sparkling water, for there is "water, water, everywhere." The old ocean casts up its treasures, and the sunlight gives all a permanent blessing.

But to the beach—the whitest, grandest ocean-platform in the land. The great Atlantic rolls to your very feet, and, bowing in a cloud of foam, pays a

majestic homage to "The City by the Sea." I wheel farther on to Sachuest Beach, and just before going down to the beach I turn off to the right and am soon on Purgatory Rocks. A romantic place indeed! As I look at the rugged sides and dangerous height, it is easy for my imagination to picture lovers' leaps, hair-breadth escapes, and the thousand and one tragedies which fiction if not reality has plentifully woven into its yawning chasm. Leaning on my " Expert," I view the land and water. 'Tis a glorious sight. Before me the Atlantic, its smooth surface dotted with an hundred sails, the whole glistening in an immense crystal panorama; behind me old Newport just awaking from a breezy night, I am happy; and even the saddest of men could not remain within himself before the ruddy, smiling face of Nature.

The exercise of my wheel has strengthened my body and cleared my mind. As do my brother wheelmen, I have taken the advice of Pope, and

" Learn from the beast the physic of the field."

The sun is my hearthstone, the ocean my toilet, the dew my diamonds, the whole world my riding-park, and the bicycle my companion. Like the tide, I wait for no man. I and my "steed" are one, with a friendship as settled as the rubber tire.

Grand old Newport, you have drained Nature's cup of blessings till you are filled, and more than filled, with all that she can give. I hear the breaking of the waves beating a solemn basso of strength and power. The sun has risen clear over the waters, and here on Purgatory I leave the reader, for from these rocks one can see and choose the best from an ever-open storehouse, the Newport of the world, blessed with

" The Solemn Benediction of the Sea."

A tail end.

Hertsberg & Harman,

Real Estate Brokers and Auctioneers,

295 Fifth Avenue,

Between 30th and 31st Sts., New York.

Parties in search of furnished or unfurnished houses and apartments will do well to communicate with us.

Special attention to Auction Sales of Household Furniture.

Telephone Call 320, 39th.

Newport Villa Owners and Cottage Rentals, for 1883.

Austin I. J., South Carolina, DeBlois', Catherine st. and Gibbs av.

Adams T. M., N. Y., Cadwallader's, Bellevue av. [Catherine st.

Ayer Mrs. J. C., New York, Brinley's,

Auchincloss Mrs. J. W., N. Y., Washington st.

Auchincloss H. B., N. Y., Washington st. [av.

Almon A. B., Salem. Mass., Red Cross

Andrews Frank W., Boston, Maple av.

Agassiz Prof. Alex., Cambridge, Mass., Castle Hill. [and Cliffs.

Astor John Jacob, N. Y., Bellevue av.

Austin Mrs. John A., N. Y., Townsends, Kay and Brinley sts.

Astor W., N. Y., Bellevue av. and Cliffs.

Anderson E. J., N, Y., Cottage st.

Appleton Thos. G., Boston, Catherine st.

Appleton Nathan, Boston, Catherine st.

Arnold Mrs. Samuel G., Providence, East shore, Middletown. [av.

Ashhurst W. H., Philadelphia, Bellevue

Angell E. G., Providence, Washington st. [tage.

Atterbury J. F., N. Y., No. 7 Cliff cot-

Ball Geo. H., Worcester, Mass., Breese's, Francis st. and Everett place.

Binney William, Providence, Bush's, Ayrault st.

Bull C. M., N. Y., near two-mile corner.

Bell Dr. C. M., N. Y., Wilson's, Narragansett av.

Barger Samuel F., N. Y., Baldwin's, Bellevue av. [av.

Beckwith N. M., N. Y., King's, Bellevue

Brown George S., Baltimore, Andrew's, Bellevue av.

Belmont O. H. P., N. Y., "Oakland," Portsmouth.

Beach Fred O., N. Y., The Whitehall.

Belmont Perry, N. Y. (not decided.)

Bowdoin G. S., N. Y., Davis' Swiss chalet, near Bailey's beach.

Bosworth F. J., Milwaukee, Oehre Point.

Bookstaver H. W., N. Y., Purgatory rd.

Bell Isaac. Jr., N. Y., Bellevue av. and Perry st.

Baker Mrs. Richard, Jr., Boston, Bellevue av. and Ledge road.

Bates C. F., N. Y., Coddington av.

Barker Wm., Providence, Paradise av.

Barker Fred., Providence, Paradise av.

Brown Stephen, Boston, Spring st.

Barstow D. H., Boston, East shore, Portsmouth.

Bryer Benjamin, N. Y., near Mianti-nomi hill. [vue av.

Brown Mrs. John C., Providence, Belle-

Bruen Mrs. M. L., Boston, Bellvue av.

Bonaparte Col. J. N. B., Baltimore, Harrison av.

Baldwin C. C., N. Y., Bellevue and Narragansett avs.

Bigelow J. R., Boston, Washington st.

Brewer Mrs. Gardner, Boston, Bellevue av. near Bailey's Beach.

Blatchford Mrs. R. M., N. Y., Greenough place and Beach st.

Blatchford Judge Samuel, N. Y., Greenough place.

Belmont August, N. Y., Bellevue av. and Cliffs. [st.

Bigelow Mrs. J. W., N. Y., Washington

Bacon Daniel B., N. Y., near Lawton's Valley.

Bancroft George, Washington, D. C., Bancroft av. and Cliffs.

Brownson J. S., Elizabeth, N. J., Washington st.

Bassett William, London, Fales', near two-mile corner.

Ballou W. M., Providence, Douglass', Conanicut Island.

Buell Mrs. Jas., N. Y., Pell's, Francis st.

Ball Charles H., Newburgh, N. Y., Case's, Everett place.

Booth Edwin. N. Y., near Paradise.

Breese Mrs. K. R., Conanicut Island.

Bishop Mrs., N. Y., Muenchinger's, Bellevue av. [on the Cliffs.

Bowler S. M., Cincinnati, Livingston's,

Bennett J. S., N. Y., Cliff cottage hotel.

Bend Geo. H., N. Y., Sargent's, Rhode Island av. [Island av.

Bird Mrs. O. W., N. Y., Potter's, Rhode

Clews Henry, N. Y., Bryce's, Bellevue and Narragansett avs.

Craven Engineer H. S., U. S. N., Heap's, Bedlow av.

Concklin H. R., U. S. engineer corps, Grant's, Bay View av.

Chickering Mrs. T. E., Boston, Willow Bank cottage.

Coles W. F., N. Y., Bellevue av. [st.

Cook Rev. Dr., N. Y., Ruggles', Spring

Clark B. S., N. Y., Woods', Bellevue av.

Coats James, N. Y., Carey's, Narragansett av.

Coleman Samuel, N. Y., Red Cross av.

Coles Mrs. E. U., N. Y., Bellevue av.

Churchill Capt. C. C., U. S. A., Ayrault st.

Caswell J. R., N. Y., Bull st.

Channing Dr. W. F., Providence, Tuckerman av.

Cleveland Dr. C., N. Y., Retirement rd.

Cook H. H., N. Y., Bellevue av. near Bailey's Beach. [Kay sts.

Caldwell Misses, N. Y., Ayrault and

Cushing Thos. F., Boston, Bellevue av.

Cullum Gen. G. W., U. S. A., Sea View av. near beach.

Chickering Chas. F., N. Y., Bellevue av.

Cunningham Dr. E. L., Boston, Cottage and Redwood sts. [mile corner.

Cook Mrs. J. J., Providence, near two-

Collins George, N. Y., Cottage st.

Colford S. J., N. Y., Hunter-Babcock cottage, DeBlois av.

Crate Mrs. M. A., N. Y., Ayrault st.

Clift Smith, N. Y., King-Wetmore cottage, Parker av.

Cox Newton, N. Y., Muenchinger's, Bellevue av. [av.

Catlin Mrs., N. Y., Fadden's, Bellevue

Clough Mrs., N. Y., Tompkins', Catherine st. and Greenough place.

Dick F. A., Philadelphia, Wheeler's, Bath road. [R. I. av.

DeRenne Mrs., Savannah, Ga., Lieber's,

Dyer Dr. E., Philadelphia, Cooper's, Bellevue av.

Dale Thos. N., Patterson, N. J., Gibbs av. and Buena Vista st. [Island.

Derby Lt. R. C., U. S. N., Conanicut

Dickey H. T., N. Y., Wellington av.

Deas Mrs., N. Y., Easton's Point. [av.

DeHauteville F. S. G., N. Y., Bellevue

Davis Theo. M., N. Y., Ocean av.

Ellis John W., N. Y., Morton's, Bellevue av.

Ellis Misses, N. Y., Francis', Francis st.

Eustis Mrs. F. A., Boston, Gibbs av.

Edgar William, N. Y., Beach st.

Eustis Prof. H. S., Cambridge, Mass., Conanicut Island.

Emmons Mrs. E. W., Boston, Channing av. and Catherine st.

Eldredge Mrs. Julia H., N. Y., Lawrence and Ruggles avs.

Evans Jonathan, Philadelphia, Peckham's, Paradise av. [st.

Elliot Lt.-Col. G. H., U. S. A., Thames

Fletcher Joseph, Providence, Titus', Broadway.

French Francis O., N. Y., Hallidon hill.

Fearing Henry S., N. Y., Annandale rd.

Fearing W. H., N. Y., Fadden's, Bellevue av.

Foster John, Boston, LeRoy av.

Francis Rev. Lewis, Brooklyn, Honeyman hill. [Cliffs.

French Abel, N. Y., Bellevue av. and

Ford John R., N. Y., Harrison av.

Ferrell J. L., Philadelphia, Conanicut Island.

French S. B., N. Y., Cliff av.

Fellows Cornelius, N. Y., Ferguson's, Hallidon hill.

Francklyn C. G., N. Y., Sands', Ledge road and Ocean av. [Cliff av.

Ferguson George A., N. Y., Chanler's,

Fell R. D., Philadelphia, Smith's, Bellevue av. and Gordon st. [av.

Furey Dr., Philadelphia, Terry's, Gibbs

Fosdicks Mrs. C. B., N. Y., Wood's, Bellevue av. [ragansett av.

Greene Mrs. J. C., N. Y., Pinard's, Nar-

Geiard Mrs., N. Y., Pinard's Narragansett av. [Channing av.

Gibbs Major Theo. K., N. Y., Wheeler's

Gibbs Miss Emily O., N. Y., Rhode Island av. and Beach st.

Gibb Miss Sarah B., N. Y., Gibbs av.

Goelet Robert, N. Y., Narragansett av. and Cliffs. [Webster st.

Goelet Ogden, N. Y., Lawrence and

Gould W. P., Major U. S. A., Mitchell's Friendship st. [Kay st.

Goelet Mrs. Sarah, N. Y., Griswold's

Gibert Mrs. A., N. Y., Bellevue av.

Gibbs Prof. Walcott, Cambridge, Mass., Gibbs av.

Gray Miss M. E., N. Y., Narragasett av.

Greene C., Providence, Coanicut Island.

Gray Mrs. G. G., N. Y., Acosta's, Ochre Point. [Park.

Gray S. M., Providence, Conanicut

Gardner Rathbone, Providence, Conanicut Park.

Gammell Prof. William, Providence, Narrangsett av. and Cliffs.

Gammell R. H. I., Providence, Narragansett av. and Cliffs.

Greene W. B., N. Y., Broadway and Malbone road.

Griswold J. N. A., N. Y., Ocean av.

Grunhut Mrs. J., N. Y., Harrison av. and old Fort road. [Bellevue av.

Gallia Count G., Philadelphia, Blight's,

Gibbes Mrs. Thos. S., N. Y., Case's, Kay st.

Gratz L. C., Philadelphia, Smith's, Bellevue av. and Gordon st. [Kay st.

Guion D. F., Baltimore, Griswold's,

Haven G. G., N. Y., King's, Bellevue av.

Hopkins Capt. Alfred, U. S. A., DeBlois', Cranston av.

Hazard Benjamin I. Georgetown, S. C., Tilley's, Malbone av.

Hacker William, Philadelphia, Anthony's, Conanicut Island.

Hazen Gen. W. B., U. S. A., two Hammett cottages, Conanicut Island.

Hayward Miss, N. Y., Fadden's, Bellevue av.

Hall P. D., N. Y., Powell's, Ayrault st.

Hone Robert S., N. Y., Spring st.

Hoyt H. S., N. Y. Beach st. and Sunnyside place. [corner.

Hazard Rowland N., N. Y., one mile

Howe Mrs. Julia Ward, Boston, Lawton's Valley. [Ayrault sts.

Hayward Mrs. M. A., Boston, Kay and

Howard Mrs. E. W., N. Y., Kay and Bull sts.

Hatch A. S., N. Y., Kay st.

Hosack Mrs. C. B., N. Y., Harrison av.

Huntington Prof. J. P., Hartford, Indian av.

Hoffman Miss Susan O., N. Y., Bellevue av. and Cliffs. [geshall aves.

Hall Peleg, N. Y., Bellevue and Coggeshall aves.

Homans E. C., N. Y., Gould Island.

Havemeyer Theo. A., N. Y., Bellevue and Coggeshall aves.

Hewitt A. S., N. Y., (not decided.)

Hartshorn Mrs. E. G., Providence, Hallidon hill.

Hunt Richard M., N. Y., Bellevue av.

Hunnewall Hollis, N. Y., Yznaga av.

Hodgson J. M., N. Y., LeRoy av.

Howland Meredith, N. Y., Knight's, Bellevue av.

Howland S. S., N. Y., (not decided.)

Hargreaves George, Denver, Nursery cottage, Middletown. [View av.

Inman John H., N. Y., Hoppin's, Beach

Ingersoll Harry, Philadelphia, Reef Point and Cliffs. [road.

Josephs Lyman C., N. Y., Purgatory

Jones Mrs. Mary M., N. Y., Wellington av.

Jones Mrs. G. F., N. Y., Harrison av.

Jones Miss Frances, N. Y., Catherine st.

Jones Frederick, N. Y., Harrison av.

Jessup Morris K., N. Y., Kane's, Bellevue av.

Jay Augustus, N. Y., Derby's, Kay st.

Keene James R., N. Y., Burn's, Hazard av.

Kennedy Miss Rachel L., N. Y., McCurdy's, Hallidon hill.

Kennedy Robert Lennox, N. Y., Russell's, Narragansett av.

Kidder J. H., Washington, Gardner's, Conanicut Island. [mile corner.

Kimber A. M., Philadelphia, near one

King LeRoy, N. Y., Spring and King sts.

King Mrs. Edward, N. Y., Spring and King sts. [Cliffs.

Knower John, N. Y., Bellevue av. and

Kane Walter L., N. Y., Wormeley's, Red Cross av. [st.

Kettletas Mrs. Eugene, N. Y., Webster

King David, N. Y.. Bellevue av. and Bowery st. [st.

Kendall Mrs. S. A., N. Y., Washington

Kernochan James P., N. N., Marine av.

Kennedy Mrs., Baltimore, Gray's, Narragansett av. [Island.

Luce C. S., Boston. Green's, Conanicut

Ludlum Mrs. S. P.. Baltimore, Brown's lane, Middletown. [Ochre Point.

Langdon Walter. N. Y., Pendleton's.,

Lusk Dr. W. T.. N. Y. (not decided.)

Lippitt Henry. Providence, Conanicut Park.

Lorillard Pierre. N. Y., Ochre Point.

Low Josiah O., Brooklyn, Castle Hill.

Low A. A., Brooklyn, Castle Hill.

Lyman Miss. Boston, Webster st.

Livingston Maturin, N. Y., Bellevue ct.

Livingston Herman T., N. Y., Sea View av. and Cliffs.

Lewis Walter H., N. Y., Ochre Point.

LeRoy Daniel, N. Y., Bellevue av.

LeRoy Stuyvesant, N. Y., Mann av.

Ledyard Mrs. Henry, N. Y., Catherine st.

Lafarge John, N. Y., Sunnyside place.

Lieber Mrs. M., N. Y., Conanicut Island.

Lord Thomas, N. Y., Cottrell's, Conanicut Island. [cottage.

McCagg Mrs. C. O., N. Y., No. 5 Cliff

Mills Ogden, N. Y., McKay's. Marine av.

McStea Nelson, New Orleans, No. 3 Pinard cottage. [av.

Mott J. L. B., N. Y., Bruen's, Bellevue

Mangum Mrs. W. P., Hunter house. Washington st. [4 Cliff cottage.

Mitchell Dr. S. Weir, Philadelphia, No.

Morgan Rev. Dr. W. F., N. Y., Hunt's, Ayrault st. [Gibbs av.

Mason Dr. J. J., N. Y., Catherine st. and

Mitchell Mrs. Mary A., Utica, N. Y., Francis st. and Everett place.

Mahony John H., N. Y., Bellevue av.

Marquand Henry G., N. Y., Rhode Island av. and Buena Vista st.

Mason Misses, Boston, Buena Vista st. and Bath road. [Bellevue av.

Miller Geo. M., N. Y., Ledge road and

Mayer Edward, N. Y., Middletown.

Miller W. S., N. Y., Bellevue av. [av.

Matthews A., N. Y., Tucker's, Yznaga

Morris Henry G., Philadelphia, Washington st.

Montgomery T. J., Boston, near Spouting Rock. [Island.

Morris Wistar, Philadelphia, Conanicut

Marvin Gen. Selden E., Albany, N. Y., Howland's, Conanicut Island.

Morris Mrs. Francis, Rhode Island av.

Mandeville Lord, England, DeBlois's, Gibbs av. and Francis st.

Merritt George W., N. Y., Bellevue av.

Mott Thos., Philadelphia, Rutherford's, Harrison av. [Catherine st.

Morgan Edwin D., N. Y., Blatchford's,

Mortimer Stanley, N. Y., The Berkley.

Morgan D. O. P., N. Y., Potter's, Rhode Island av. [ington st.

Morris Miss Jane, Philadelphia, Wash-

Metcalf Emmons, Boston, Downing's. Malbone av.

Maynard Mrs. Horace, Knoxville, Tenn., Gardner's, Conanicut Island. [place.

Nash Mrs. H. J., Providence, Everett

Neilson Mrs. M. N., N. Y., Cottage st.

Newton Henry, Erie, Pa., Marlboro st.

Neilson Fred., N. Y., Boit's, Beach st.

Oelrichs Charles M., N. Y., Seymour's, Kay st. [gansett av.

Oothout William, N. Y., King's, Narra-

O'Donnell Mrs. H. C., Carroll Manor, Maryland, Ochre Point. [vue av.

Otis Mrs. James, N. Y., Fadden's, Belle-

Parker Dr., U. S. N., Hazard's, Catherine st. [vue av.

Post Edwin A., N. Y., Cooke's, Belle-

Post William, N. Y., Pomeroy's, Bellevue av. [road and Cliffs.

Pruyn J. V. L. Albany, Chanler's, Bath

Prince Mrs., Boston, Willow Bank cottage. [st.

Palmer Mrs. Fanny, Philadelphia, Beach

Phillips M. S., Brooklyn, Carroll av.

Parsons Geo. M., Cincinnati, Hazard's, Francis st. and Rhode Island av.

Porter F. B., Hartshorn's, Hallidon hill.

Pond Mrs. Harriet N., N. Y., Harrington's, Ayrault st.

Pond A. Phelps, N. Y. (not decided.)

Paul J. W., Philadelphia, Tatum's, Washington st. [Pelham st.

Paine John W., Troy, N. Y., Marshall's,

Pumpelly Prof. R., Gibbs av.

Padelford Edward M., Philadelphia, Bellevue av.

Pierson J. F., N. Y., Bellevue av.

Perry Mrs. C. G., Philadelphia, Greenough place. [Cherry st.

Paull W. W., Philadelphia, Second and Cherry st.

Powell Dr. S. C., New Haven, Beach st.

Pugh Rev. J. H., New Haven, Indian av.

Phelps Royal, N. Y., Clay and Dixon sts.

Philbrick Edward S., Boston, Coddington Point.

Pell Mrs. Waldron, N. Y., Greenough pl.

Post Mrs. L. F., N. Y., Bellevue av.

Pumpelly Prof. R., Transcontinental Survey, Swinbourne's, Greenough pl.

Phinney Theo. W., Chicago, Carroll av.

Parkman Geo. F., Boston, Bellevue av.

Peterson Chas. J., Philadelphia, Bath rd.

Potter Edward T., N. Y., Catherine st.

Potter R. B., N. Y., Stevens's, Rhode Island av.

Pratt Samuel F., Boston, Bellevue av.

Robinson Dr. Beverly, N. Y., Carry's Bath road. [Everett place.

Read Gen. Meredith, Paris, Little's.

Rives Dr. W. C., Jr., Boston, Red Cross av. [st.

Rives G. L., N. Y., Tompkins, Redwood.

Roberts Mrs. Marshall O., N. Y., Anthony's, Bellevue av. and the Cliffs.

Roebling Col. W. A., Brooklyn, Mayers. Washington st. [av.

Remsen R. G., N. Y., Lyman's, LeRoy

Robbins H. A., N. Y., Willing's, Catherine st.

Rhett Mrs. E. P., Baltimore, Conanicut Island.

Russell C. H., N. Y., Narragansett av.

Rosengarten G. D., Philadelphia, Case's, Catherine st. [av.

Robbins G. A., N. Y., Arnold's, R. I.

Rogers Archibald, N. Y., Cushing's, near Spouting Rock.

Rives W. C., Boston, Red Cross av.

Richards W. T., Germantown, Pa., Conanicut Island.

Rice Henry A., Boston, Washington st.

Rhinelander Frederic W., N. Y., Redwood st.

Rogers Mrs. W. B., Boston, Gibbs av.

Rogers Prof. Fairman, Philadelphia, Nugents's, Coggeshall av.

Rogers Maxon, Boston, East Shore.

Starr Dr. L., Philadelphia, Smith's, Washington st. [tage.

Sampson Henry, N. Y., No. 1 Cliff cottage.

Stokes A. M., N. Y., Howland's, Conanicut Island. [vue av.

Swan F. C., N. Y., Muenchinger's, Bellevue av.

Schott Mrs. Ellen L., N. Y., Cranston av.

Shepard Mrs. E. A., Providence, Stockton's, Bellevue av. [Cliff cottage.

Sellers William, Philadelphia, No. 2

Shoemaker B. H., Philadelphia, Conanicut Island. [av.

Skinner Francis L., Boston, Red Cross av.

Stevens John A., N. Y., Rhode Island av.

Shields Prof. C. W., Princeton, N. J., Ochre Point.

Stanard Mrs. M. A., Baltimore, Bull st.

Seymour Mrs. C. M., N. Y., Kay st.

Stout F. A., N. Y., Bellevue av. and Cliffs.

Swift Mrs. H. W., N. Y., Bellevue av.

Stitt Seth B., Philadelphia, Bellevue av. and Pelham st. [and Jones avs.

Stevens Mrs. Paran, N. Y., Bellevue

Stout Mrs. A. G., N. Y., Bellevue ave. and cliffs.

Sands Mrs. A. L., N. Y., Greenough Place and Catherine st.

Steadman Lt. Com., U. S. N., Pelham st.

Shipley Murray, Cincinnati, Washington st.

Sanford M. H., N. Y., Washington st.

Schermerhorn E. H., N. Y., Narragansett ave.

Sherman W. W., N. Y., Shephard and Victoria avenues. [ave.

Slater J. W., Providence, Narragansett

Smith Rev. Dr. Cotton, N. Y., Chanler's, Cliff av.

Simmons Prof. W. C., Boston, Beach View av.

Sandford John, N. Y., The Whitehall.

Sandford W. C., N. Y., The Whitehall.

Smith Rev. J. T., D. D., N. Y., (not decided.) [st.

Smith B. R., Philadelphia, Washington

Sturtevant Eugene, Boston, Indian ave.

Smith Henry J., Providence, Bellevue court. [ave.

Sigourney Mrs. M. B., Boston, Bellevue

Sheldon Frederic, N. Y., Annandale Road and Narragansett ave.

Thompson Frank, Philadelphia, Cliff Cottage Hotel.

Turnure Lawrence, N. Y., Cushman's, Rhode Island ave. and Catherine st.

Thurlow S. L., Wilkesbarre, Pa., Francis's, Conanicut Island. [ley av.

Tefft W. E., N. Y., Whitwell's, Berke-

Townsend Mrs. Isaac, N. Y., No. 2 Pinard cottage, Narragansett av.

Tillinghast W. M., N. Y., No. 1 Pinard cottage, Narragansett av. [av.

Thurber F. B., N. Y., Clarke's, Parker

Townsend Gen. Fred., Albany, Cram's, Paradise av. [vue court.

Tyler Sidney F., Boston, Peet's, Belle-

Ticknor Mrs. George, Boston, Eyre's, Beach st. [and DeBlois avs.

Terry Rev. R., Peekskill, N. Y., Gibbs

Tooker G. M., N. Y., Kay and Touro sts.

Tooker Miss Mary, N. Y., Bellevue av. and Perry st. [Washington st.

Taylor Rear Admiral, U. S. N., Hunter's.

Tilton Samuel G., Boston, Sunnyside court.

Thorn W. K., N. Y., Narragansett av.

Tailer Mrs. Henry A., N. Y., Bellevue av.

Travers W. R., N. Y., Narragansett av.

Tyler George F., Philadelphia, Bellevue court. [gles av.

Tennant D. B., Petersburg, Va., Rug-

Thayer Nathaniel, Boston, Bellevue av.

Torrance Daniel, N. Y., Bellevue av.

Thorndike Mrs. G. H., N. Y., Church and High sts.

Taylor H. A. C., N. Y., Annandale rd.

Vanderbilt Cornelius, N. Y., Tucker's, Yznaga av. and Cliffs. [View av.

Van Rensselaer, Mrs. A., N. Y., Beach

Vanderbilt W. K., N. Y., Train's, Bellevue av. near Bailey's beach.

Van Brunt Mrs. Judge, Brooklyn, Bull's, near two-mile corner.

Van Alen J. J., N. Y., Clay st. [av.

Wilde Miss E. G., Boston, Rhode Island

Weir Dr. Robert F., N. Y., Biddle's, Rhode Island av. [tages.

Weston Mrs. F. A., N. Y., Shore cot-

Wilson Mrs. H. C., N. Y., Finch's, High st. [cottage, Narragansett av.

Winthrop B. R., N. Y., No. 3 Pinard

Winans Ross R., Baltimore, Castle hill.

Ware F. M., Boston, East Shore, Portsmouth. [mouth.

Ware W. R., Boston, East Shore, Ports-

Wales George W., Boston, Yznaga av. and the Cliffs.

Wright H. A., N. Y., Rhode Island av.

Whitehouse W. F., Chicago, Rhode Island av. [ault st.

Worden Rear Admiral, U. S. N., Ayr-

Weld W. G., Boston, Bellevue av.

Whipple John, N. Y., Sea View av.

Willoughby H. L., Philadelphia, Coddington point. [hill.

Witherbee Silas H., N. Y., Honeyman

Willard E. W., Chicago, Beach View av.

Wetmore George Peabody, N. Y., Bellevue av.

Watson Dr. W. A., N. Y., Spring st.

Whiting Mrs. S. S., N. Y., Webster st. and Bellevue av.

Whiting Augustus, N. Y., Bellevue av.

Wilson Prof. J. H., N. Y., Cottage and Redwood sts. [st.

Winn Mrs. A. E., Philadelphia, Cherry

Wolfe Miss C. L., N. Y., Ochre point.

Willing R. L., Philadelphia, Red Cross av. [road.

Wheeler Charles, Philadelphia, Bath

Warren G. H., N. Y., Narragansett av. and Clay st. [av.

Weld Mrs. W. F., Boston, Narragansett

Winthrop E. L., Boston, Bellevue av.

Woodworth Mrs. A. P., N. Y., Retirement road.

Wharton Joseph L., Philadelphia, Conanicut Island.

Wharton C. W., Philadelphia, Conanicut Island.

Wharton Job, Philadelphia, Conanicut Island. [Island.

Webster Sidney, N. Y., Griswold's, Bellevue av. [av.

Watson C. W., N. Y., DeBlois's, Gibbs

Wheatland S. G., Lowell, Mass., No. 6 Cliff cottage. [Island.

Wise Mrs. J. C., Gardner's, Conanicut

Yardley Mrs. Jane, Philadelphia, Rhode Island av.

Distances to Prominent Places in and around Newport.

FROM STATE HOUSE TO	Miles.
Stone Bridge. by East Road	11 68
Glen	6 29
Centre Third Beach	4 05
Centre Sachuest Beach	3 48
Centre Easton's Beach	1 49
Purgatory	2 72
Paradise Rocks	3 51
Fort Adams. Parade via Thames st. and Wellington ave.	3 77
Around Neck. via Thames st. and Wellington ave. by outer road. Ocean and Bellevue aves. back to Court House	10 69
Spouting Rock via Thames	2 63
Boat House via Bellevue around Parade	2 98
Miantinomi Hill	1 52
Pirate's Cave. near Bateman's by outer road, past Mr. Bronson's residence	4 28
Bristol Ferry. East road	11 55
Bristol Ferry, West road	10 92

FROM COMMERCIAL WHARF	
Nearest wharf. Fort Adams	0 90
Rose Island wharf	1 37
Goat Island wharf	0 43

ALONG THE CLIFFS FROM BATH ROAD TO	
Narragansett avenue	0 61
Marine avenue	1 41
Boat House (total length of Cliff Path)	2 77

FROM OCEAN HOUSE	
Beginning of Cliff on Bath road	0 78
Boat House via Bellevue ave.	2 25

LENGTH OF	
Conanicut in a straight line	8 02
The Island of Rhode Island in a straight line	15 85
Goat Island from the Light House to the southern point	0 74
Easton's Beach in a straight line	0 54
Sachuest Beach in a straight line	1 22

WIDTH OF	
Conanicut in a straight line	8 00
Island of Rhode Island	3 02

FROM WICKFORD WHARF TO	
North end Prudence Island	8 24
South end Prudence Island	6 36
Quonset Point	2 31
North end Conanicut Island	3 78
Beaver Tail Light	8 70

FROM WARWICK LIGHT TO	Miles
North Point of Prudence Island	1 72
North Point of Conanicut Island	6 34
South Point of Popasquash Island	4 12
Beaver Tail Light	14 84
Naytt Light	4 47

FROM BRISTOL FERRY LIGHT TO	
North Point of Prudence Island	4 64
South Point of Prudence Island	5 63
South Point of Popasquash Neck	2 07
Mount Hope Point	1 89
Rocky Point wharf	6 20
Slade's Ferry (greatest length of Mount Hope Bay)	7 63
Fall River Turnpike. Warren (length of Bristol Neck)	6 04

FROM NORTH END GOULD ISLAND TO	
South end Prudence Island	2 84

FROM NORTH POINT CONANICUT ISLAND TO	
South end Prudence Island	2 84

DISTANCES BY ROAD, ISLAND OF RHODE ISLAND, FROM BRISTOL FERRY WHARF TO	
Court House, Newport, by East road	11 55
Court House. Newport, by West road	10 92
Centre Easton's Beach. shortest road	12 22
Centre Sachuest Beach, shortest road	11 25
Centre Third Beach, shortest road	11 63
Purgatory	11 13
Paradise Rocks	10 75

HEIGHTS, NARRAGANSETT BAY, ABOVE HIGH-WATER MARK.	Feet.
Quaker Hill. Island of Rhode Island	280 00
Mount Hope	217 00
Barker's Heights, the highest point, western shore of Bay, west of road from Wickford to Narragansett Pier	200 00
Crotch lightning-rod, house of Henry Bull, Esq., Newport	180 95
Highest point, Prudence Island	170 00
Miantinomi Hill, base of U. S. Coast Survey signal	157 75
Highest point, Conanicut Island	130 00
Top of cupola, house of Theodore W. Phinney, Esq.	111 05
Telegraph Hill	102 43

Time of High Water at Newport, R. I., 1883.

	JUNE.	JULY.	AUG.	SEPT.
1	4 18 P.M.	5 05 P.M.	6 22 A.M.	7 30 A.M.
2	5 22	6 08	7 13	8 10
3	6 24	7 05	7 58	8 49
4	7 21	7 52 A.M.	8 41	9 30
5	7 48 A.M.	8 27	9 23	10 12
6	8 41	9 10	10 06	10 56
7	9 35	9 57	10 50	11 41
8	10 28	10 44	11 33	12 25 P.M.
9	11 19	11 28	12 14 P.M.	1 11
10	12 05 P.M.	12 10 P.M.	12 57	1 58
11	12 47	12 50	1 40	2 50
12	1 28	1 31	2 28	3 48
13	2 09	2 14	3 21	4 48
14	2 54	3 02	4 20	5 47
15	3 42	3 55	5 20	6 45 A.M.
16	4 33	4 53	6 17	7 08
17	5 26	5 49	6 44 A.M.	7 56
18	6 18	6 17 A.M.	4 33	8 46
19	7 07	7 08	8 20	9 40
20	7 30 A.M.	7 56	9 09	10 36
21	8 17	8 43	10 00	11 34
22	9 05	9 33	10 54	12 30 P.M.
23	9 54	10 23	11 48	1 23
24	10 46	11 14	12 41 P.M.	2 17
25	11 36	12 05 P.M.	1 35	3 13
26	12 24 P.M.	12 55	2 31	4 08
27	1 11	1 46	3 32	5 02
28	2 02	2 43	4 33	5 51
29	2 57	3 45	5 32	6 37
30	3 58	4 51	6 24	7 18
31		5 53	7 09	

To find the time of High Water at the following places add to the time of High Water at Newport the figures opposite the names:
Providence, 0 29 | Warren, 0 29 | Wickford, 0 11 | Nantucket 4 53 | Greenwich, 0 17
Fall River, 0 25 | Edgartown, 4 31 | Vineyard Haven, 3 58 | Nayatt Point, 0 05 | Bristol, 0 20
To find the time of High Water at the following places subtract from the time of High Water at Newport the figures opposite the names:
Beaver Tail, 0 01 | Point Judith, 0 13 | Block Island, 0 31.

Officers Stationed at Fort Adams, R. I.

Major — Charles B. Throckmorton, commanding Post and Light Battery B.
Colonel — James W. Scully, Post Quartermaster.
Assistant Surgeon — Richard Barnett, Post Surgeon.
First Lieutenant — Alexander B. Dyer, Regiment and Post Adjutant and Regimental Treasurer.
Captain Frederick Fuger, Regimental Quartermaster, Post Treasurer and Ordinance Officer.
Major — George B. Rodney, commanding Battery B.
Captain — Edward Field, commanding Battery L.
Captain — Arthur Morris, commanding Battery G.
Major — John W. Roder, commanding Battery F.
Captain — William Ennis, commanding Battery D.
First Lieutenants — George G. Greenough (L), Samuel R. Jones (G), Sidney W. Taylor (L), William Everett (B), Leverett H. Walker (G), Charles A. L. Totten (B), George L. Anderson (E).
Second Lieutenants — Clarence Deems (G), Howard A. Springett (B), Walter S. Alexander (B).

MRS. C. DONOVAN,

Of 315 Fifth Avenue, New York,

Has opened at her

BRANCH HOUSE, CASINO BLOCK,

NEWPORT,

AND IMPORTS A ....

Large Variety of the Latest Novelties,

DURING THE SEASON.

Ladies should avail themselves of the opportunity presented to dress in the latest fashion.

Officers U. S. Torpedo Station, Newport, R. I.

RANK.	NAME.	RANK.	NAME.
Capt.	Thos. O. Selfridge.	Lieut.	Washburn Maynard.
Lieut.-Com.	R. B Bradford.	P. A. Paymaster.	Stephen Rand, Jr.
" "	A. G. Caldwell.	Gunner.	John R. Grainger.
" "	T. F. Jewell.	Lieut.-Com.	John S. Newell.
Lieut.	J. L. Hunsicker.	Pay Clerk.	Orlando Tabor.
"	T. C. McLean.		

Torpedo Class, 1883.

RANK.	NAME.	RANK.	NAME.
Commander.	C. E. Clark.	Lieut.	H. R. Tyler.
"	Wm. B. Hoff.	Surgeon.	J. B. Parker.
"	D. W. Mullan.	Lieut.	John Hubbard.
Lieut.	Albert Ross.	"	Frederic Singer.
"	Chas. A. Adams.	"	W. H. Reeder.
"	H. C. T. Nye.	Ensign.	T. A. Park.
"	Martin E. Hall.	"	A. G. Rogers.
Ensign.	Louis Duncan.	Lieut.	A. B. H. Lillie.
Lieut.	C. H. Judd.	"	C. K. Curtis.
"	N. C. Barnes.	Ensign.	P. V. Lansdale.
Commander.	R. P. Leary.	"	S. K. Reynolds.
Lieut.	J. D. Adams.		

Churches.

African Methodist Episcopal Church, Bellevue ave., next to Jewish Cemetery.
All Saints Episcopal Church, Beach, cor. Cottage street.
Central Baptist Church, Clark street.
Channing Memorial Church, Pelham street, opp. Touro Park.
Church of the Holy Name of Mary, Our Lady of the Isle (R. C.), Spring, cor. Levin street.
Emanuel Church (Episcopal), Spring, cor. Dearborn street.
First Baptist Church, Spring, cor. Sherman street.
First Methodist Episcopal Church, Marlboro' street, near Charles.
First Society of Friends, West Broadway and Marlboro' street.
Second Baptist Church, cor. North Baptist and Farewell streets.
Shiloh Baptist Church (colored), Mary street, cor. School.
Thames Street M. E. Church, Thames street, cor. Brewer.
Trinity Church (Episcopal), Spring street, cor. Church.
Union Congregational Church, Division street, between Church and Mary.
United Congregational Church, Spring and Pelham streets.
Zion Church (Episcopal), Touro street, south side of Mall.

The Streets and Avenues of Newport.

Allan's Court, 18 Spring.
Annandale Road, Narragansett avenue to Bath road.
Ann Street, Thames to Spring.
Anthony, Bowery to Pope.
Appleby Avenue, Farewell to Green Lane.
Arnold, Broadway to Summer.
Atlantic, now Ward avenue,
Ayrault, Broadway to Catharine.
Batchelder's Court, Spring near Lee avenue.
Bancroft Avenue, Bellevue avenue to Coggeshall avenue.
Barney, Spring to Whitfield court.
Bateman Avenue, Carroll avenue to Coggeshall avenue.
Bateman Avenue, Ocean avenue to Winans avenue.
Bath Road, Bellevue avenue to bathing beach.
Battery, Third to the bay.
Bay View Avenue, Warner to Broadway.
Beach, Bellevue Avenue to R. I. av.
Beach View Avenue, Mile Corner to Green End.
Beacon, Hillside av. to Main Road.
Bedlow Av., Broadway to Malbone av.
Bellevue Avenue, Touro to Ocean av.
Bellevue Court, Bellevue avenue near Perry.
Berkeley, R. I. avenue to Cranston.
Berkeley Avenue, Bellevue avenue to Annandale road.
Berkeley, Wellington avenue, south.
Bliss Mine Road, Bliss road to water works.
Bliss Road, Broadway to Indian av.
Boss Court, Wellington avenue,
Bowery, Spring to Annandale road.
Bradford Road, Butler to DeWolf.
Branch, Broadway to West Broadway.
Brenton Avenue, Ocean avenue to Castle Hill avenue.
Brenton, Thames to Spring.
Brewer, Thames to Spring.
Bridge, Thames to Washington.
Brinley, Kay to Catherine.
Broadway, Washington sq. to 1 Mile Cor.
Buena Vista, R. I. av. to Channing av.

Bull, Broadway to Kay.
Burnside Av., Warner to W. Broadway.
Butler, Gibbs to Rutgers.
Byrnes Court, Lee avenue to Thames.
Caleb Earl, Broadway to W. Broadway.
Callender Av., Warner to W. Broadway.
Cannon, Thames to Spring.
Carroll Avenue, Thames to Ocean av.
Castle Hill Avenue, Ocean avenue to Harrison avenue.
Catherine, Bellevue av. to Channing avenue.
Central Court, 12 Bull.
Channing Avenue, Kay to Bath Road.
Channing, Hall av. to Malbone av.
Charles, Washington square to No. Baptist.
Cherry, Third to the Bay.
Chestnut, Third to the Bay.
Church, Thames to Bellevue avenue.
Clarendon or Deblois Court, Bellevue avenue to State.
Clarke, Washington square to Mary.
Clay, Narragansett avenue to Dixon.
Cliff Av., Bath road to Sea View av.
Clinton Av., Warner to Broadway.
Coddington Avenue, Malbone avenue to Sunset avenue.
Coddington, Thames to Farewell.
Coggeshall Av., Spring to Bellevue av.
Collins, Broadway to W. Broadway.
Collins Avenue, Bliss road to Beach View avenue.
Commercial Wharf, foot Franklin.
Connection, Thames to Wilbar av.
Corne, Mill to Prospect Hill.
Cottage, Beach to Catharine.
Cottage Place, from Beach st., south.
Cotton's Court, 124 Thames.
Covell, Farewell to Edward.
Cranston Avenue, Broadway to Kay.
Cranston, Broadway to Cranston av.
Cross, Bridge to Poplar.
Davis Court, Callender avenue to Burnside avenue.
Deblois (Clarendon) Court, Bellevue avenue to State.
Dearborn, Thames to Spring.
Deblois Avenue, Kay to Catharine.

Dennison, Thames to Spring.
DeWolf, Hall avenue to Rutgers.
Division, Mill to Touro.
Dixson, Thames to Bellevue avenue.
Downing, Bellevue avenue to State.
Duke, Washington square to Marlborough.
East, Pope, south.
East Bowery, continuation Bowery.
Edgar Court, Bath Road.
Edward, Broadway to White.
Elizabeth, north from Catharine.
Elm, Cross to the Bay.
Evarts, Hall avenue to Butler.
Everett Place, southeast from Kay.
Extension, Thames, east.
Fair, Thames to Spring.
Farewell, 2 Broadway to Long lane.
Fillmore, Wellington av. to Harrison avenue.
Fillmore Court, east from Brinley.
Fir, Catharine to Beach.
Fountain, Spring to Anthony.
Francis, Ayrault to R. I. avenue.
Franklin, Thames to Spring.
Frank, Thames to Spring.
Freebody, East Bowery to Bath Road.
Friend, Edward to Green lane.
Friendship, Broadway to Gibbs av.
George, Pelham to Mill.
Gibbs Av., Bath road to Broadway.
Gibbs, Malbone av. to Long lane.
Golden Hill, Spring to Thomas.
Gidley, Thames to Spring.
Gordon, Bellevue av. to Coggeshall avenue.
Gould Court, east from Broadway.
Gould, Warner to Broadway.
Grafton, Thames, west.
Grant Court, Perry, north.
Greene Avenue, Hall av. to Malbone avenue.
Green Lane, Warner to W. Broadway.
Greenough Place, Beach to Ayrault.
Green, Thames to Spring.
Gurney Court, north from Cherry.
Hall Avenue, Warner to DeWolf.
Halsey, Gibbs to Rutgers.
Hammond, Thames to Spring.
Harrison Av., Ocean av. to Old Fort road.
Hayden Court, Bath Road.
Hazard Avenue, Bellevue avenue to Coggeshall avenue.
Heath Court, Spruce.

High, Church to Touro.
Hillside Av., Bedlow av. to Sunset av.
Holland, Thames to Spring.
Homer, Gibbs to Rutgers.
Houston Av., Wellington av. to Connection.
Howard Avenue, Broadway to Kay.
Howard, Thames to Spring.
Hozier, Park Place to Spring.
John, Spring to Bellevue avenue.
Johnson Court, Spruce.
Jones Avenue, Bellevue av. to King.
Kay, Touro to Channing avenue.
Kilburn Court, Broadway.
King, William to Bowery.
King, Wellington avenue to old Fort road.
Lawrence Avenue, Webster to Marine avenue.
Ledge Road, Bellevue avenue to Boat House.
Lee Avenue, Thames to Spring.
Leroy Avenue Bellevue av. to Ochre Point av.
Leroy Place, Parker av. to Bowery.
Levin, Spring to Bellevue avenue.
Lincoln, R. I. av. to Cranston av.
Linden Place, east from Lincoln.
Long Lane, Farewell, north.
Long Wharf, Thames to the Harbor.
Madison Place, south from Walnut.
McAllister Court, Spring near Dixon.
Maher Ct., Spring near Wheatland av.
Maitland Court, Third, east.
Malbone Avenue, Broadway to Coddington avenue.
Mann Avenue, Broadway to Kay.
Marlborough, Thames to Broadway.
Marine Avenue, Bellevue av. to Lawrence avenue.
Marsh's Court, 79 Thames.
Marsh, Third to Washington.
Martin, John to Prospect Hill.
Mary, Thames to Touro.
Meeting, Washington square to Marlborough.
Melville Court, 78 Thames Street.
Miantonomi Avenue, Broadway to Hillside avenue,
Miantonomi Place, north from Malbone avenue.
Middleton, Dixon to Bath road.
Milburn Court, 282 Thames.
Mill, Thames to Bellevue avenue.

Mount Vernon Court, continuation of Mt. Vernon street.
Mount Vernon, Touro to Bull.
Narragansett Av., Thames to Cliffs.
New, Broadway to Malbone avenue.
Newport Av., Warner to Broadway.
Norman, Redwood av. to water works.
North Baptist, Thames to Farewell.
North Kay, Kay to Bliss road.
Oak, Broadway to West Broadway.
Ocean Avenue, Bellevue avenue to Castle Hill avenue.
Ochre Point Avenue, LeRoy avenue to Ruggles avenue continued.
Old Fort Road, Brenton to King.
Park Place, Touro to Broadway.
Park, Broadway to Gould.
Parker Av., Bellevue av. to Annandale road.
Pelham, Thames to Bellevue avenue.
Perry, Spring to Bellevue avenue.
Pine, Third to the Bay.
Pleasant, Warner to Broadway.
Pond Av., Warner to W. Broadway.
Pope, Thames to East.
Poplar, Farewell to the Bay.
Potter, Thames, west.
Prescott Hall Road, Gibbs to Rutgers.
Price Neck Av., Ocean av. to Harrison av.
Prison, Washington sq. to River lane.
Prospect Hill, Thames to Bellevue av.
Redwood Av., Kay to Catharine.
Redwood Place, Spring, near Pope.
Redwood, Bellevue av., to Cottage.
Retirement Road, Middleton to Cliff avenue.
Red Cross Av., Bath road to Beach Street.
R. I. Av., Broadway to Bath Road.
River Lane, Charles to Marlborough.
Ruggles Avenue, Carroll av. to Ochre Point.
Sanford, Thames to Farewell.
School, Church to Touro.
Seaview Avenue, Cliff av. to Cliffs.
Second, Marsh to Battery.
Sharon, Thames, west.
Sheffield Av., Hall av. to Malbone av.
Shepard Avenue, Bellevue avenue to Lawrence avenue.
Sherman Court, 69 Thames.
Sherman, Spring to Mount Vernon.
Simmons, west from Thames.
South Baptist, Thames, east.

Spring, Broadway to Coggeshall av.
Southmayd, Hall avenue to Butler.
Spruce Court, Spruce.
Spruce, Vicksburg place to W. Broadway.
State, Beach to Clarendon Court.
Stockholm, Thames, west.
Stone, Broadway to Spring.
Summer, Malbone av. to Broadway.
Sunnyside Court, east of Third.
Sunnyside Place, South of Beach.
Sunset Av., Main road to the Bay.
Tew's Court, Beach, south.
Thames, Farewell to Brenton.
Third, Marsh, north to Newport Asylum.
Thomas, Golden Hill to John.
Tilley Avenue, Gibbs, south.
Touro Court, Washington sq. south.
Touro, Spring to Bellevue avenue.
Underwood Court, Thames, east.
Vernon Av., Broadway to Bliss road.
Vicksburg Place, Spruce to Gibbs.
Victoria Court, Coggeshall avenue to Lawrence avenue.
Walnut, Farewell to the Bay.
Wanton, Coddington to N. Baptist.
Ward Avenue, Clay to Annandale rd.
Warner, Farewell to Malbone av.
Washington Square, Thames to State House.
Washington, Long wharf, north.
Weaver Av., Freebody to Annandale road.
Webster, Thames to Cliffs.
Wellington Av., Thames to Fillmore.
West Broadway, Marlborough to Broadway.
West, Pope to Perry.
Wetmore Av., Shepard av. to Marine avenue.
Wheatland Avenue, Bellevue avenue to Coggeshall avenue.
White, Farewell to Green Lane.
Whitfield Court, Touro, north.
Wilbar Avenue, Wellington av. to Connection.
William, Spring to Bellevue avenue.
Willow Court, Thames, near Pope.
Willow, across Third to the Bay.
Winans Avenue, Harrison av. to Ocean av.
Young, Thames to Spring
Yznaga Avenue, Bellevue av., east.

JOHN E. LEDDY,

HORSE  SHOER,

No. 7 Farewell Street,

Newport, R. I.

Particular Attention paid to Gents' Driving Horses.

Blocks, Buildings, Halls, Etc.

Abrahams Block, Bellevue avenue, opposite Bath road.
Aquidneck Hall, Mill, Cor. Corne.
Armory Hall, Clarke.
Butler's Block, Bellevue avenue, corner John.
Casino Building, Bellevue avenue, near Bath road.
City Hall, Thames, cor. Long wharf.
Coddington Block, 341 Thames.
Cottrell's Block, 222 Thames.
Custom House, Thames, cor. Franklin.
DeBlois Block, Bellevue avenue.
Downing's Block, Bellevue avenue, corner Downing. [Kay.
Fludder's Block, Bellevue avenue, cor.
Gas Co.'s Building, 175 to 181 Thames.
Helme's Block, 76 Spring. [School.
Home for Friendless Children, 12

Horgan's Block, Bellevue avenue, opposite John.
Liberty Block, 16 Farewell.
Masons Hall, School, cor. Church.
Newport Reading Room, Bellevue avenue, corner Church.
Newport Hospital Building, Howard avenue, near Broadway.
Odd Fellows Building, 20 Washington square.
Opera House, Washington square.
Post-Office Building, Thames, corner Franklin.
Queen Anne B'ld'g, 71 and 73 Thames.
Redwood Library and Athenaeum, Bellevue avenue, corner Redwood.
State House, Washington square.
Travers Block, Bellevue avenue, corner Bath road.

U. S. Gunnery Training Ship "Minnesota."

Captain JAMES H. GILLIS.
Lieut.-Commander GEO. T. DAVIS.
Lieutenant JAMES M. MILLER.
" ARTHUR P. NAZRO.
Master BRADLEY A. FISKE.
Ensign FRANK E. BEATTY.

Ensign ROBERT M. DOYLE.
Surgeon JAMES S. KNIGHT.
Passed Asst. Surgeon WM. H. RUSH.
" Engineer L. W. ROBINSON.
" " STACY POTTS.
Paymaster GEORGE E. HENDEE.

Chaplain RICHARD HAYWARD.

Officers of U. S. Training Ship "New Hampshire."

Commander CHARLES E. CLARK.
Lieutenant F. M SYMONDS.
" JOHN V. B. BLEECKER.
" SUMNER C. PAINE.
" JAS. W. GRAYDON.
" BOYNTON LEACH.

Master GEO. H. WORCESTER.
Ensign BENJAMIN TAPPAN.
" HENRY MINNETT.
Paymaster JOHN FUREY.
P. A. Surgeon JOHN C. WISE.
Chaplain HENRY H. CLARK.

Assistant Surgeon JAMES D. GATEWOOD.

Places of Amusement.

Newport Opera House, Washington square.
Casino, Bellevue avenue.
Westchester Polo Grounds, end of Thames street.

OFFICERS.

—OF—

THE NEWPORT CASINO,

For the Years 1882-83.

President.
AUGUST BELMONT.

Vice-President.
WILLIAM R. TRAVERS.

Secretary.
EDWARD B HARRINGTON.

Treasurer.
GEORGE R. FEARING.

COMMITTEES.

House Committee.
FREDERIC W. STEVENS, Chairman
DAVID KING,   C. C. BALDWIN,
THOMAS F. CUSHING,   HENRY S. FEARING.

Games.
WILLIAM R. TRAVERS, Chairman.
HOLLIS HUNNEWELL, FREDERIC W. STEVENS,
N. THAYER. JR.

Entertainments and Theatricals.
THOMAS F. CUSHING, Chairman.
OGDEN GOELET,   FAIRMAN ROGERS.
N. THAYER. JR.

By-Laws.
DAVID KING, Chairman.
HENRY S. FEARING,   FREDERIC W. STEVENS.

Governors.
WILLIAM R. TRAVERS,   )
AUGUST BELMONT,   ) Term expires
THOMAS F. CUSHING,   ) August, 1883.
DAVID KING.   )

HENRY S. FEARING,   )
PIERRE LORILLARD,   ) Term expires
OGDEN GOELET,   ) August, 1884.
NATHANIEL THAYER, JR.   )

GEORGE R. FEARING,   )
FAIRMAN ROGERS,   ) Term expires
JOHN N. A. GRISWOLD,   ) August, 1885.
CHRISTOPHER C. BALDWIN.)

HOLLIS HUNNEWELL,   )
W. WATTS SHERMAN,   ) Term expires
JAMES G. BENNETT,   ) August, 1886.
FREDERIC W. STEVENS.   )

Casino Stockholders.

	Shares.		Shares.
Agassiz. A.	1	Lawrence, F. C.	1
Andrews, C. A.	2	Ledyard, L. Cass	1
Appleton. T. G.	1	Lorillard, Louis L.	1
Astor, J. J.	2	Lorillard, Pierre	2
Astor, W. W.	2	Low, A. A.	2
Astor, William	2		
		Manice, W. D. F.	1
Baker, Mrs. Ellen	1	Marin, M. C.	1
Baker, Richard	1	Marquand, Henry G.	2
Baldwin, C. C.	1	Miller, G. M.	1
Baldwin, C. H.	1	Morgan, Edwin D.	2
Barber, T. H.	1	Morton, L. P.	2
Barger, Sam'l F.	1		
Beach, C. N	1	Norman, G. H.	1
Beckwith, N. M.	1		
Bedlow, Henry	1	Oelrichs, Herman	1
Bell, Isaac. Jr.	2		
Belmont, August	2	Phelps, Royal	2
Bennett, J. G.	32	Phoenix, S. W.	1
Brown, G. S.	1	Pierson, J. F.	1
Bryce, Carroll	1		
Bryce, J. S.	2	Rives, Wm. C.	1
		Rodman, S. W.	1
Codman, M. P. R.	1	Rogers, Fairman	2
Colt, C H.	1		
Cooper, Edward	1	Sanford, A. Wright	1
Corbin, Austin	2	Sands, Mahlon	1
Cushing, R. M.	1	Schuyler, Philip	1
Cushing, T. F.	2	Sheldon, Fred.	1
Cutting, R. L. Jr.	1	Schell, Aug.	2
		Sherman, W. W.	1
D'Hautville, F. S. G.	1	Stevens, F. W.	4
Douglass, W. P.	2	Stevens, H. L.	1
		Stillman, James	2
Ellis, J W.	1	Stokes, Anson Phelps	2
		Stout, F. A.	2
Fearing, G. R.	2	Stuyvesant, Rutherf'd	1
Fearing, H. S.	2		
French, F. O.	1	Thayer, N. Jr.	2
French, S. B	1	Thayer, E. V. R.	1
		Tooker, G. M.	1
Gammell, Prof. Wm.	1	Travers, John, Jr.	1
Garrett, Robert	1	Travers, Wm. R.	2
Goelet, Ogden	2	Travers, Wm. R. Jr.	1
Goelet, Robert	1	Tweedy, Edmund	1
Gray, H. W.	1	Tyler, George F.	1
Griswold, J. N. A.	2		
		Van Alen, J. H.	1
Havemeyer, T. A.	2	Van Buren, T. C.	1
Honey, S. R.	1	Vanderbilt, C.	2
Howland, G. G.	1	Vanderbilt, W. K.	2
Hunnewell, Hollis	2		
Hunt, R. M.	1	Wales, G. W.	1
		Warren, George H.	2
Ingersoll, Harry	1	Weaver, J. G.	1
Inman, J. H.	1	Weld, W. F. Jr.	1
		Weld, W. G.	1
Keene. J. R.	2	Wetmore, G. P.	2
Kennedy, R. L.	1	Whipple, John	1
Kernochan, J. Fred.	1	Whiting, Sarah	1
King, David	1	Wilson, R. T.	2
Knower, John	1	Winthrop, E. L.	1
		Wolfe, C. L.	1
Latrobe, F. C.	2	Woodward, J. T.	1

NEWPORT OMNIBUS COMPANY.

BROADWAY LINE.

Omnibuses of the Broadway line leave the post-office hourly, on every week day, from 7 A. M. to 9.15 P. M., and the one mile corner every hour from 7.30 A. M. to 9.45 P. M.

BELLEVUE AVENUE LINE.

On and after Thursday, June 14th, an omnibus will leave Washington square at 7.30, 9, 10.30 A. M., 12 M., 12.30, 2, 3.30, 5, 7 P. M.; leave end of avenue at 8.15, 9.45, 11.15 A. M., 12.45. 1.15, 2.45 4.15, 5.45, 7.45 P. M.

CABS.

Cabs at low rates may be engaged by leaving orders at Travers block, or at office of N. Y. & B. Express Co., 175 Thames street. Telephone connection.

RAILROAD AND STEAMBOAT

TIME TABLES.

SUMMER ARRANGEMENT, 1883.

OLD COLONY RAILROAD.

On and after June 18th trains

LEAVE NEWPORT

For **Boston** 7.45, 10.15 a.m., 2.55, 4.30 p.m. Return 8.15, 11.40 a.m., 3.35, 4.45 and 6.00 p.m.
For **Coal Mines** 7.20, 10.15 a.m., 2.55 p.m. Return 9.04, 10.42 a.m., 2.01, 5.51 p.m.
For **Bristol Ferry** 7.20, 10.15 a.m., 2.55, 4.30 p.m. Return 8.59, 10.38 a.m., 1.56, 5.47 p.m.
For **Tiverton** 7.20, 7.45, 10.15 a.m., 2.55, 4.30 p.m. Return 8.54, 10.32 a.m., 1.50, 5.33, 5.42 p.m.
For **Fall River** 7.20, 7.45, 10.15 a.m., and 2.55 4.30 p.m.
For **Taunton** (Dean street) 7.20, 7.45, 10.15 a.m., 2.55 p.m. (Wales street) 4.30 p.m.
For **Middleboro'** (via Weir Junction) 7.45 a.m. Return 3.35 p.m.; via Taunton 10.15 a.m., 2.55 p.m. Return 6.55, 9.06 a.m.; (via Myricks) 4.30 p.m.
For **Cape Cod** 7.45 a.m., 2.55 p.m.
For **Plymouth** 2.55 p.m.
For **New Bedford** 7.45, 10.15 a.m., 4.30 p.m.
For **Providence** 7.45, 10.15 a.m., 2.55 p.m.
For **Fitchburg and Stations on Northern Division** 7.45, 10.15 a.m., 2.55 p.m.
Lowell 2.55 p.m.
For **Oak Bluffs**, 7.45, 10.15 a.m., 2.55 p.m.
For **Nantucket** 10.15 a.m.

—:o:—

OLD COLONY STEAMBOAT CO.

NEWPORT TO NEW YORK.

Fall River Line.

Steamers PILGRIM and BRISTOL leave daily (Sundays included), at 8.45 p.m. (Sundays at 9.45 p.m.)

Newport Line.

Steamers OLD COLONY and NEWPORT leave daily (Sundays excepted) 9.05 p.m.

Staterooms and Tickets can be secured at the New York & Boston Despatch Express Co.'s Office, Newport Gas Light Co.'s Building, 475 Thames street.

—:o:—

FOR CONANICUT ISLAND.

JAMESTOWN AND NEWPORT FERRY

On and after Monday, May 7, 1883, the steamer JAMESTOWN will run as follows:—
Leave Jamestown 6.15, 8.45, 10.30 a.m., 1.00, 3.30, 6.00 p.m.
Leave Newport 7.00, 9.45, 11.30 a.m., 2.30, 4.30, 6.45 p.m.

SUNDAYS.

Leave Jamestown 9.30 a.m., 12.15, 5.00 p.m.
Leave Newport 10.15 a.m., 12.45, 5.45 p.m.

—:o:—

NEWPORT AND WICKFORD RAILROAD AND STEAMBOAT COMPANY.

Steamer EOLUS leaves Commercial Wharf, Newport, four times daily, as follows:—

At 7.00 a.m., connecting at Wickford with trains for Kingston, Westerly, Stonington, New London, Hartford, New Haven, and New York; also with trains due at Providence at 9.10 and Boston 10.50 a.m. Arrive at New York 4.22 p.m.

At 12.00 m., connecting with Shore Line Express for New London, New Haven and New York; also with trains for Hartford, Springfield, Albany and the West, and with train due in Providence at 2.10. Passengers arrive in New York at 6.40 p.m.

At 5.00 p.m., connecting with express leaving New York at 1.00 p.m., due at Providence at 7.03 p.m., and Boston at 8.50 p.m.

At 11.10 p.m., (Sundays included) connecting with night mail due in New York at 6.30 a.m.

RETURNING,

WILL LEAVE WICKFORD JUNCTION:

At 4.25 a.m., (Sundays included) connecting with night mail from New York at 10.00 p.m., and due in Newport at 6 a.m.

8.35 a.m. On arrival of train from New London and Stonington, Westerly and Kingston, for Wickford and Newport, also Kingston Special from Providence 7.40 a.m., arriving at Newport at 9.50 a.m.

1.35 p.m. On arrival of connecting train leaving New York at 8.05 a.m., Stamford, New Haven, New London, Stonington, Westerly and Kingston; also with trains leaving Providence at 12.10 p.m. Arrive at Newport at 2.50 p.m.

6.27 p.m. On arrival of Shore Line express train leaving New York at 1.00 p.m. Due in Newport at 7.45 p.m.

Connecting with Providence four times daily, viz.: from Newport at 7.00 a.m., 12.00, 5.00, and 11.10 p.m.; from Providence at 12.00 m., 7.40 a.m., and 12.10 and 5.30 p.m.

*Express trains to and from New York will not stop at Belleville or Wickford.

—:o:—

CONTINENTAL STEAMBOAT CO.

NEWPORT, CONANICUT PARK, ROCKY POINT AND PROVIDENCE.

Leave Newport week days at 7.30 a.m. and 4.30 p.m.; returning, leave Providence at 9.00 a.m. and 4.00 p.m. Sundays at 8.00 a.m., 12.00 m., and 5.00 p.m.; return at 10.00 a.m., 2.30 and 6.00 p.m.

Excursion tickets to Providence and return 60 cents.

Children under 12 years, 30 cents.

The morning boat from Newport Tuesdays and Fridays stops at Prudence Island both ways.

—:o:—

NEWPORT AND BLOCK ISLAND.

Steamer GEORGE W. DANIELSON makes daily trips Sunday excepted to Block Island, leaving Newport at 12.30 p.m., and Block Island at 8.00 a.m., connecting with steamers to and from Providence, and with boats and trains to and from New York, weather permitting.

Location of Fire Alarm Boxes.

FIRST WARD.

Box 12. Cor. Third and Poplar streets.
Box 14. Cor. Thames and Poplar streets.
Box 15. O. C. R. R. Steamboat wharf.
Box 16. Cor. Cherry and Second streets.

SECOND WARD.

Box 21. Lake's Corner, Broadway.
Box 23. Corner Broadway and Marlborough streets.
Box 24. Cor. Brinley and Kay streets.
Box 26. Cor. Broadway and Malbone av.
Box 27. Cor. R. I. av. and Catharine st.
Box 28. Cor. Gould and Warner streets.
Box 29. Cor. Kay st. and Everett place.

THIRD WARD.

Box 3. City Hall.
Box 31. Police Station.
Box 34. Cor. Spring and Mary streets.

FOURTH WARD.

Box 4. Cor. Bellevue av. and Downing street.
Box 41. Cor. Spring and Franklin sts.
Box 42 Cor. William and Thomas sts.
Box 43. Cor. Bath road and Cliff av.

FIFTH WARD.

Box 5. Cor. Thames street and Brown and Howard's wharf.
Box 51. Cor. Thames street and Lee av.
Box 52. Cor. Bellevue and Narragansett avenues.
Box 53. Cor. East Bowery and Freebody streets.
Box 54. Cor. Bellevue and Bancroft avs.
Box 56. Cor. Bellevue av. and Ledge road.
Box 57. Cor. Coggeshall and Wheatland avenues.

Carriage Fares.

For each passenger from one place to another between the northern boundary line and the southern side of Narragansett avenue . . . . . 50 cts.
For each passenger carried beyond the above-mentioned limits, first mile, or fraction of mile, additional . . . . 50 cts.
And every mile, or part of a mile, thereafter . . . . 25 cts.
For a child, when accompanied by an adult, NO CHARGE.
Each passenger entitled to transportation of one Trunk without charge.
Each additional Trunk, Valise, Traveling Bag, Carpet Bag, Bundle, Basket, etc., a charge of ten cents to be made.
Carriage or Hack, $2.00 for first hour, $1.50 for each subsequent hour.

Wharves.

Aquidneck Mill wharf, 293 Thames.
Bowen's wharf, 189 Thames.
Brown & Howard's wharf, from 269 Thames.
Bull's wharf, 129 Thames.
Coddington wharf, 331 Thames.
Commercial wharf, 219 Thames.
Cottrell's wharf, 253 Thames.
Engs' wharf (now called Lopez wharf), 137 Thames.
Ferry wharf, 175 Thames.
Hammett's wharf, 241 Thames.
Kinsley's wharf, 199 Thames.
Langley's wharf, 221 Thames.
Lee's wharf, 283 Thames.
Long wharf, 59 Thames.
Lopez wharf, 137 Thames, (formerly Engs' wharf.)
Peckham's wharf, 145 Thames.
Perry Mill wharf, 235 Thames.
Sayer's wharf, 209 Thames.
Scott's wharf, 213 Thames.
Sherman's wharf, 95 Thames.
Sisson's wharf, 311 Thames.
Spring wharf, 303 Thames.
Swan's wharf, 85 Thames.
Swinburne's wharf, 143 Thames.
Wait's wharf, 319 Thames.
Williams' wharf, changed to Brown & Howard's wharf, 269 Thames.

NEW YORK YACHT CLUB.

OFFICERS, 1883.

Commodore: JAMES D. SMITH.
Vice Commodore: ANSON PHELPS STOKES.
Rear-Commodore: EDWARD M. BROWN.
Secretary: CHARLES A. MINTON.
Treasurer: JAMES O. PROUDFIT.
Measurer: CHALES H. HASWELL.
Fleet Surgeon: MORRIS J. ASCH, M. D.

Regatta Committee.
JOHN H BIRD, *Chairman.*
CHESTER GRISWOLD.   J. FREDERIC TAMS.

House Committee.
T. B. ASTEN. *Chairman.*
H. N. ALDEN.   ELIJAH A. HOUGHTON, *Secretary.*
B. C. CLEEMAN.   THE SECRETARY, *Ex-Officio.*

Committee on Admissions.
WILLIAM H. THOMAS. *Chairman.*
F. W. J. HURST, *Sec'y*   JOHN S. DICKERSON.
WILLIAM E. ISELIN.   OGDEN GOFLET.

MEMORANDA.

CLUB HOUSE - - - - - 27th Street, cor. Madison Avenue.
SECRETARY'S OFFICE - - - - - - - - - Club House.
TREASURER'S OFFICE - - - - - - - - Club House.
MEASURER'S OFFICE - - - - Post Office Box 2961, N. Y. City.
STATION - - - - - - - - - - New York.

(BY SPECIAL APPOINTMENT.)
Telegraphic Night Signals.
WILLIAM F. COSTON - - - - - - - 15 State Street, Room 35.
Yacht Flag Maker.
S. W. WOLF - - - - - - - - - Southampton. Eng.
Buttons, Braid, Ornaments, etc.
RAYMOLD & WHITLOCK - - - - 39 West 14th Street, New York.

THE INTERNATIONAL CODE OF SIGNALS HAS BEEN ADOPTED BY THE CLUB.

List of Schooners belonging to the N. Y. Yacht Club, 1883.

NAME.	OWNERS.	PORT.	NAME.	OWNERS.	PORT.
Schooners.			*Schooners.*		
Alarm.	G. L. Kingsland.	N. Y.	Clio.	E. E. Chase.	N. Y.
Albatross.	E.W.Humphreys	"	Clochette.	C. W. Galloupe.	Boston.
Ambassadress	William Astor.	"	Ciytie.	A. B. Cook.	Cowes.
Aroostook.	H. C. Sturges.	"	Clytie.	A. Phelps Stokes.	N. Y.
Eolus.	Sam'l A. Wood.	"	Columbia.	J. Lester Wallack	"

Breech-Loading Yacht Gun "Admiral."

4 SIZES. THE BEST GUN METAL.

No. 1, 17 inches, No. 10 Shell,	-	-	$ 75.00	No. 3, 28 inches, No. 3 Shell,	- - $175.00
No. , 24 " " 4 "	-	-	125.00	No. 4, 32 " " 2 "	- - 200.00

Cartridges loaded to order. This is the finest Gun ever offered to Yachtsmen. Simple in construction, absolutely SAFE. Handsome in finish. No Yacht is complete without one.

Call and see samples at

Yacht Emporium, 43 Milk Street, G. F. Clarke & Co., Sole Agents for Boston.

Muzzle-Loading Yacht Guns.

17 inches, No. 10 Shell,	-	-	$55.00	28 inches, No. 3 Shell,	- - $135.00
24 " " 4 "	-	-	99.00	32 " " 2 "	- . - 160.00

These Guns are finished in every detail equal to the Breech-Loaders.

YACHT EMPORIUM.

G. F. CLARK & CO.,

YACHTS AND VESSELS

SOLD ON COMMISSION. AGENTS FOR

Crockett's Spar Varnish, Haggerty's Patent Slide for Masts.

Yacht Fittings of all Kinds, Yacht Tenders.

ALL CLASSES OF YACHTS FOR SALE, AND TO CHARTER.

43 MILK STREET, BOSTON.

Branch Office, - - - . - - 83 South Street, New York.

Schooners.

NAME.	OWNERS.	PORT.
Comet.	W. H. Langley.	N. Y.
Crusader.	J. R. Maxwell.	"
Dauntless.	Caldwell H. Colt	"
Ellie.	Lawrence Pike.	"
Estelle.	James D. Smith.	"
Fiona.	E. Boutcher.	P'rtsm'th, Eng.
Fleetwing.	R. S. Elliott.	Y. Y.
Fortuna.	H. S. Hovey.	Boston.
Frolic.	Chas. C. Haight.	N. Y.
Grayling.	Latham A. Fish.	"
Halcyon.	Chas. J. Paine.	Boston.
Hermes.	Dan'l Appleton.	N. Y.
Intrepid.	Lloyd Phoenix.	"
Lotos.	Wm. A. Cole.	"
Louisa.	N. P. Rogers.	"
Madeleine.	J. S. Dickerson.	"
Meta.	Franklin Dexter.	Boston.
Mischief.	C. R. Gill, M. D.	N. Y.
Montauk.	Sam'l R. Platt.	"
Nokomis.	W. A. W. Stewart	"
Norseman.	Ogden Goelet.	"
Palmer.	R. Stuyvesant.	"
Peerless.	F. Hathaway.	N. Bedf'd.
Phantom.	E. V. S. Thayer.	Boston.
Princess.	Jesse Metcalf.	Prov.
Rambler.	W. H. Thomas.	N. Y.
Republic.	Henry J. Steere.	Prov.
Resolute.	A. S. Hatch.	N. Y.
Ruth.	H. Hathaway.	"
Sappho.	Prince Sciarra.	Naples.
Seminole (yawl)	A. E. Douglass.	N. Y.
Siren.	E. R. Washburn.	"
Social.	{ Henry Lippitt. / C. W. Lippitt. }	Prov.
Sylph.	Geo. H. Chase.	N. Y.
Tioga.	H. W. Perkins.	"
Varuna.	Geo. H. B. Hill.	"
Vesta.	Fred. F. Ayers.	"
Vif.	C. A. Stevenson.	"
Wanderer.	E. D. Morgan.	"
Water Witch.	C. H. Mallory.	"
Wave Crest.	E. N. Dickerson.	"
Whistler.	R. S. Elliott.	"

Sloops.

NAME.	OWNERS.	PORT.
Active.	C. P. Horton.	Boston.
Bedouin (cutter)	Arch'd Rogers.	N. Y.
Breeze.	H. P. Kingsland.	"
Christine.	H. E. Dodge.	"
Coming.	Steph'n Peabody	"
Elaine.	H. G. Russell.	Prov.
Ethel.	J. Gillelan, Jr.	N. Y.
Fanita.	George J. Gould.	"
Fanny.	John D. Prince.	"
Gracie.	{ Chas. R. Flint. / Jos. P. Earl. }	"
Hildegard.	Herm'n Oelrichs.	N. Y.
Iola.	Oswald Jackson.	"
Julia.	E. M. Brown.	"
Kelpie.	J. N. Winslow.	"
Medusa (cutter)	Franklin Dexter.	Boston.
Mischief.	J. R. Busk.	N. Y.
Mona (cutter)	E. M. Padelford.	Newp't
Mystery.	W. B. Parsons.	N. Y.
Orion.	Geo. C. Cooper.	"
Oriva (cutter)	C. Smith Lee.	"
Pocahontas	{ J. D. Smith. / H. Oelrichs. }	"
Regina.	Ralph N. Ellis.	"
Rover.	Wm. E. Iselin.	"
Sagitta.	Henry C. Ward.	"
Vindex (cutter)	Arthur W. Blake.	Boston.
Vision.	J. J. Alexandre.	N. Y.
Vixen.	F.C.Lawrance,Jr	"
Waif.	Gov. Kortright.	"
Winona (cutter)	James Stillman.	"
Whileaway.	G. F. Randolph.	"
Whitby.	Joseph Park.	"
Wizard.	Caldwell H. Colt.	Hartf'd
Building.	R. B. Hartshorne.	N. Y.

Steamers.

NAME.	OWNERS.	PORT.
Camilla.	F. Brandreth.	Sing Sing.
Corsair.	J. P. Morgan.	N. Y.
Eirena.	W. J. Carmichael	"
Emu.	A. H. Barney.	"
Ermengarde.	G. P. Russell.	"
Faustine.	G. P. Russell.	"
Fauvette.	E. Perignon.	Havre.
Fiona.	E. Boutcher.	Gr'n'ck
Freyja.	L. T. Dickson.	Phila.
Ideal.	T. J. Havemeyer.	N. Y.
Lady of the Lake.	Sir Robert Peel.	Geneva, Switz.
Lurline.	J. M. Waterbury	N. Y.
Minnehaha.	Henry I. Barbey.	Geneva, Switz.
Naja.	Geo. A. Bech.	N. Y.
Namouna.	J. G. Bennett.	"
New Amsterdam.	C. G. Gunther.	"
Ocean Gem.	Wm. P. Clyde.	"
Orienta.	J. A. Bostwick.	"
Polynia.	J. G. Bennett.	"
Promise.	Alf'd de Cordova.	"
Radha.	Pierre Lorillard.	"
Rival.	Geo. G. Haven.	"
Skipjack.	S. M. Mills.	"
Skylark.	J.Lester Wallack	"
Theresa.	J. M. Fiske.	"
Tillie.	W. H. Starbuck.	"
Vedette.	E. S. Jaffray.	"
Vision.	J. J. Alexandre.	"
Building.	Geo. S. Scott.	"

BROOKLYN YACHT CLUB.

W. R. WADSWORTH, *Secretary.*   J. M. SAWYER, *Measurer.*
JACOB M. BERGEN, *Treasurer.*   J. H. DIMON, *President.*

NAME.	OWNER.	NAME.	OWNER.
SCHOONERS.		Spry,	J. H. Dimon.
Madeline,	J. S. Dickerson.	Wayward,	J. D. Fowler.
Meteor,	A. Perry Bliven.		
Ray,	A Perry Bliven.	STEAMERS.	
SLOOPS.		New Amsterdam,	C. G. Gunther.
Genevieve,	H. S. Wood.	Tourist,	C. A. Chesebrough.
Mystery,	C. A. Chesebrough.	Virginia,	F. G. Heron.

PROVIDENCE YACHT CLUB.

BENJAMIN DAVIS, COMMODORE.

ROBERT W. JENKS, *Vice-Commodore.*   C. J. MANCHESTER, *Secretary.*
BENJAMIN STILLWELL, *President.*   H. F. THOMPSON, *Treasurer.*
ARTHUR M. BLACK, *Measurer.*

NAME.	OWNER.	NAME.	OWNER.
		CAT-RIGGED YACHT.	
SLOOPS.		Wanderer	Benjamin Davis.
		Rarus	Simon Cameron.
Hope	Edward J. Anderson.	Country Boy	E. N. Pettis.
Starlight	Robert W. Jenks.	Louise	Benjamin Davis.

WARWICK YACHT CLUB.

ANDREW ROBESON, COMMODORE.

FRED P. SANDS, *Vice-Commodore.*   HOWARD L. CLARKE, *Secretary.*
JOHN K. H. NIGHTINGALE, *R. Com.* W. C. RHODES, *Treasurer.*
JAMES N. HART, *Measurer.*
Regatta Committee: G. W. RANKIN WM. ELY, W. C. RHODES.

NAME.	OWNER.	NAME.	OWNER.
		Tahena	A. Robeson.
SCHOONERS.		Undine	H. C. Allen.
Angie	Daniel H. Barstow		
Republic	Henry J. Steere.	CAT-BOATS.	
Social	H. F. Lippitt.	Dolly	C. Rathbone.
		Halcyon	R. G. Hazard, 2d.
SLOOPS.		Meta	J. A. Renwick.
Elaine	Henry G. Russell.	Molly	Horace Binney.
Hildegarde	H. L. Clarke.	Paralos	J. W. Huntington.
Lackawanna	E. F. Lucas.	Venona	W. V. Olyphant.
Lilian	S. C. Powell.	Warwick	J. K. H. Nightingale.
Lizzie L.	F. P. Sands.	Louise	F. H. Brown.

Postal Regulations.

First-Class Matter. — *Letters.* The postage on letters not over one half oz. to all parts of the United States is 3 cts.; and for each half oz. or fraction thereof of additional weight, 3 cts. Articles sealed are charged as letters. *Postal Card*, 1 ct. *Drop, or Local Letters* (to be delivered in the office where mailed), 2 cts. a half oz., at offices where free delivery by carrier is established; at other offices, 1 ct. Paid letters not delivered at the first office named will be re-forwarded to the place where the owner is if known, or returned to the writer, if indorsed with that request, free. Letters to be mailed from one office to another will not be sent unless prepaid at least 3 cts. The domestic postal card may be sent to Canada without any extra stamp.

Second-Class Matter. — *Newspapers and Periodicals to regular subscribers.* (No limitation of weight)— When mailed from a known office of publication or news agency, and issued regularly, the postage for each pound, or fraction of a pound, is 2 cts., the matter in all cases to be weighed in bulk at the office of mailing. Newspapers, except weeklies, without regard to weight, and magazines not over 2 oz., deposited in letter-carrier offices for delivery there, 1 ct. each. Magazines over 2 oz., 2 cts.

Third Class Matter. — On *Transient Newspapers and Magazines, Books, Pamphlets,* and occasional publications, circulars, engravings, photographs, hand-bills, posters, blanks, proofsheets, manuscript copy if accompanied with proof, maps, and sheet-music, the postage on one package, to one address, is 1 ct. for every 2 oz., or fraction, the weight of the package being limited to 4 lbs., except *single* volumes of *books,* which may weigh over 4 lbs. Newspapers, except weeklies, deposited in letter-carrier offices for delivery there, require only 1 ct. each, without regard to weight; and periodicals require, if under 2 oz., 1 ct., and for any weight over 2 oz., only 2 cts. each.

Fourth-Class Matter. — Letter enve opes (whether printed or plain), cards, sample cards, plain and ornamental paper, seeds, cuttings, bulbs, roots, scions, and other articles of merchandise which are not in any way liable to injure the contents of the mail-bag, or the person of any one engaged in the postal service, 1 ct. for every oz. or fraction, the weight of the package being limited to 4 lbs. The name of the sender of any article, or the address, may be written in the package or on its outside, with the word " from " above or preceding the same, or briefly the number and names of the articles enclosed, and addresses may be either written, printed, or affixed, at the option of the sender; but any writing of the nature of a letter or personal correspondence, in or upon any article, will subject it to letter rates.*

Registration. — *All mail matter may be registered* by prepayment of a fee of 10 cts. for each address, in addition to the required postage.

Money Orders, for any amount not exceeding $300 in one day, and not exceeding $100 on one order, are issued in the principal offices, on payment of the following fees: Orders not exceeding $10, — 8 cts ; orders exceeding $10, and not exceeding $15, — 10 cts; orders exceeding $15, and not exceeding $30, — 15 cts.; orders exceeding $30, and not exceeding $40, — 20 cts.; orders exceeding $40, and not exceeding $50, — 25 cts.; orders exceeding $50, and not exceeding $60, — 30 cts.; orders exceeding $60, and not exceeding $70, — 35 cts.; orders exceeding $70, and not exceeding $80, — 40 cts.; orders exceeding $80, and not exceeding $100, — 45 cts. There are over 5,000 money-order offices.

Foreign Registration. — Letters, printed matter, and samples may be registered to most countries for a fee of 10 cts, besides the postage, which must be all prepaid.

Foreign Money Orders. — Money Orders are issued to *Great Britain* and *Ireland* for a fee of 25 cts. for amounts not over $10; for 50 cts. for amounts from $10 to $20; for 70 cts. from $20 to $30; for 85 cts. from $30 to $40; for $1.00 from $40 to $50. To *Switzerland,* for amounts not exceeding $50; the fee being 25 cts. for each $10, or fraction of $10. To *France, Germany, Italy, Canada,* and *Newfoundland,* for 15 cts. for $10, or less; and 15 cts. more for each additional $10, or fraction of $10. Foreign money orders limited to $150 in one day.

---

* It is forbidden to send in the mails to foreign countries pieces of coin, jewelry of any kind, articles of gold or silver, or anything subject to customs duty. Packages will not be forwarded at sample rates of postage, unless they are actually trade-samples, and are enclosed in such a manner as will admit of an easy examination of the contents. Articles of merchandise are expressly excluded from the mails to Canada.

POST OFFICE GUIDE.

OFFICE HOURS: 7 A. M. to 8 P. M. SUNDAYS, 7 to 9 A. M.
Lobby open from 6 A. M. to 9 P. M. SUNDAYS, 9 A. M. to 6 P. M.

OPENING AND CLOSING OF MAILS.

	Closes.		Opens.	
	a. m.	p. m.	a. m.	p. m.
New York and Southern	6.40	12.40	6.40	4.45
		5.10	10.30	
Boston, Eastern and Western States	7.00	12.40	10.30	4.45
		2.40	11.30	6.30
		5.10		
Providence, R. I.	6.40	2.40	10.30	4.45
		5.10		6.30
Fall River, Mass.	7.00	2.40	11.30	6.30
New Bedford, Mass.		7.00		6.30
Taunton, Mass	7.00	......	......	6.30
Jamestown, R. I.	11.00	......	......	3.00
Block Island. R. I.	12.00	......	......	......
Tiverton, R. I., (way mail)	8.00	......	... ..	6.00

POST OFFICE FREE DELIVERY.

Collections from all Street Letter Boxes are made as follows: at 5 A. M., 12 M., and 3.30 o'clock P. M.

Distribution by Carriers at 7 and 11 A. M., and 4. 45 P. M.

Telephone Subscribers.

Aquidneck Hotel.
Adams Express Co.
Attleton, L. F.
Andrews, Constant A.
Auchincloss, Mrs. John.
Austin. I. J.
Albro, Samuel.
Aquidneck National Bank.
Andrews, Frank W.
Ayer, J. C.
Aylesworth, Thomas.
Adams, Thatcher M.
Agassiz, Prof. Alex.

Baker, A. Prescott.
Bateman, Benjamin.
Barker, Robert S.
Barber, Charles P.
Belmont, August.
Bowker, James J.
Brown & Howard.
Bryer, Peleg.
Bracket, Dr. C. A.
Bull, Melvill.
Burton, B. J.
Bennett, James Gordon.
Bedlow, Mrs. Josephine.
Babcock, Mrs.
Brinley, Dr. E. H.
Barker, Alvin A.
Brown, James A.
Barker Bros.
Bank, Merchants.
Bank, Newport National.
Bank. Aquidneck National.
Burdick, J. Truman.
Briggs & Co.
Barney, James H.
Berkley, Thos.
Bowen, Heirs of Geo.
Barger, S. F.
Bell, Dr. C. M.
Bateman, Seth.
Binney, Wm.
Brown, James H.
Barlow, F. N.
Barlow, T. N. & Co.
Brierley, J. H.
Bedlow, Henry.
Boardman, Mrs. C.
Bull, Henry.
Bull, Henry, Jr., Residence.
Bull, Henry, Jr., Insurance office.
Burdick, A. L., Store.
Burdick, A. L., Residence.

Caswell, Massey & Co., Casino store.
Caswell, Massey & Co., Thames Street.
Caswell, Hazard & Co.
Castoff, Henry.
Curry Bros.
Curry, John J.
Carlisle, Horace.
Centennial Tea Store.
City Clerk's Office.
Cornell & Son.
Cozzens, Henry W.
Cozzens & Bull.
Cozzens, Wm. C. & Co.
Cozzens, Wm. C.
Cozzens, J. H. & Son.
Cozzens, J. H.
Cozzens, Wm J.
Cottrell, Michael, Residence.
Cottrell, Michael, Store.
Crosby, John H. Jr.
Cleveland, Dr. C.
Cushman, E. C.

Cushing, C. F.
Covell, Wm. K. Jr.
Crocker, L. F.
Clerk's Office Supreme Court.
Casino, Newport.
Curley, Dr. J. P.
Clegg, J. H. L.
Crimin & Butler.
Cliff Cottage Hotel.
Custom House.
Coleman, Samuel.
Curry, Mrs Wm.
Chickering, C. F.
Coats, James.
Chase, G. R. & J. R.
Caldwell, Towson.
Caldwell & Bacon.
Conroy, P. F. & Co.
Carr, Geo. R.
Craven. Lieut. Com.
Clarke, Bembridge.

Derby & Forsyth.
Daily News.
Davis, L. J.
Davis & Pitman.
Dunn, Tho nas.
Downing, Geo. F.
Downing, B. F. Jr.
Derby, Lie it. R. C.
DeBlois, John B.
Dickey, Judge H. F.
Davis, The o. M.

Earl & Prew's Express Co.
Eyre. Wilson.
Edgar, Com. Wm.
Ellis, John W.
Eldridge, Mrs.
Eddy, James A.

Field, Geo. B.
Fludder, Wm. & Co.
Fludder, Wm. H.
Fludder, James.
Francis, Dr. Samuel W.
Freeborn, Thomas W.
French, Francis O.
Fergusor, Geo. A.
Fearing, Wm. H.
French, S B., Residence.
French, S. B., Stable.
Faerber, Peter.
Finch, James B.
Fletcher, Joseph.
Fellows, C.
Forsyth, Russell.
Fadden, F. W. & Co.
Fearing, Geo. R.

Gas Light Co.
Gladding, Thomas.
Gratrix, George.
Greene, W m. O. & Son.
Gilpin, John.
Griswold, John N. A.
Gilliatt, Mrs. J. H.
Greene, Joan H.
Greason, Clarence.
Graves Point Fishing Club.
Gibbs, The o. K.
Goddard, Dr. P.
Gibert, Ma lam.

Harrington, E. B.
Harris, F. G.
Hass, Henry J.
Hazard, James S.
Hayward, E. & A. H.
Honey, Samuel R., Office.
Honey, Samuel R., Residence.

Howard, J. N., Residence.
Howard, J. N., Office.
Heath, H. A. & Co.
Hillside Farm.
Hodgson, J. M.
Hunnewell, Hollis.
Hoffman, Miss S. O.
Hunter, Miss S. M.
Hammond, E. S.
Hazard, J. L. & G. A.
Hardwick, Geo.
Howland, Meredith.
Hazard, Geo. M., Store.
Hazard, Geo. M., Residence.
Hospital, Newport.
Havemeyer, Theo. A.
Hudson, Henry J.
Hollins, H. B. & Co.
Howard, Mrs. E. S.
Holmes, Mrs.
Heartshorn, Mrs. I.

Ingersoll, Harry.
Inman, J. H.

Jourdon, J. H., Residence.
Jourdon, J. H., Office.
Judson, J. A., Residence.
Judson, J. A., Office.
Jones, Mrs. Geo. F.
Jay, Augustus.

Kaull, H. A.
Keene, James R.
Kernochan, James P.
Kinsley Express Co.
King, Mrs Edward.
Kennedy, Miss R. L.

Landers, Albert C., Store.
Landers, Albert C., Residence.
Langley, John S.
Langley, Wm. C.
Lawton, Geo. P.
Leonard, Geo. P.
Lineham, Geo. N.
Lieber, Mrs. F.
LeRoy, Stuyvesant.
Lamont Farm.
Ledyard, Mrs. M. C.
Little, Lieut. Wm. McCarty.
Lewis, Walter H,
LaFarge. John.
Lee Brothers.
Lawton, Mrs. Asa T.
Lewis & Tilley.
LeRoy, Daniel.
Low, H. H.
Low, J. O.
Littlefield, Geo. H.

Mason, John J.
McAdams & Openshaw.
Murray, Hiram.
Muenchinger & Son.
Millar, Geo. M.
Mercury Office.
Mason, Geo. C. & Son.
Murray, Chas. S.
McLeish, James.
Manchester, Chas. H.
McKim, Dr. W. R.
Mutual Union Telegraph Co.
Merchants Bank.
Mason, John B.
Manchester, O. C., No. Portsmouth P O.
Morris, Mrs. Com.
Metcalf, Mrs. Emmons.
Mountgomery, T. J.
Munville, Lady.

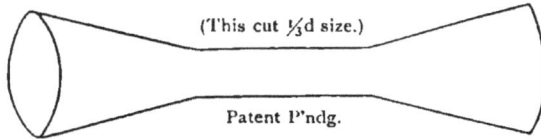

N. Y. & B. Despatch Express Office.
N. Y. & B. Despatch Express Co. Stable.
Newport Transfer Express Co.
Newport Omnibus Co.
Newport Ice Co.
Newport Laundry
Newport Laundry, Branch office J. D. Richards'.
Newport Reading Room.
Newport Casino.
Newport Mercury.
Newton Dudley, Office.
Newton Dudley, Residence.
Newport & Wickford Steamboat Co. Office.
News, Dr. Annie.
N. E. Weston Electric Light Co., H. W. Cozzens, Supt.
Newport Hospital.
Northern Trans-Continental Survey Office.
Nason, Mrs. H. B.
Newport National Bank.

Ocean House.
Ogden Farm.
Old Colony Steamboat Co.
Old Colony Boston Freight Depot.
Old Colony New York Freight Depot.
Old Colony Repair Shop.
Old Colony Passenger Depot.
Oxx, Samuel H.
Oman, R. L.
Ocean House Stable.

Perry House.
Peckham & Manchester.
Pinniger & Manchester.
Pitman, T. T.
Porter, F. B. & Co.
Perry Bros.
Pumpelly, Prof. R. U.
Police Station.
Police Telephone, Box Washington and Bridge Sts.
Police Telephone, Box Broadway and Caleb Earl St.
Police Telephone, Box Bellevue Ave. and Catherine St.
Police Telephone, Box Lee Ave. and Thames St.
Police Telephone, Box Bellevue and Bancroft Aves.
Police Telephone, Box Bath Road and Freebody St.
Prince, George.
Pray, Harley W.
Perkins, G. W.
Peckham, J. H.
Potter, Thos. J.
Pearce, B. W.
Potter, Capt. Oliver.
Post, Edwin A.

Potter, Edward,
Post, William.
Porter, F. B., Residence.
Padelford, E. M.
Pinard Cottages.

PUBLIC SCHOOL DEPARTMENT.
Supt.'s Office, Geo. A. Littlefield.
Willow Street School.
Edward Street School.
Cranston Avenue School.
Potter School.
Codington School.
Thames Street School.
Parish School.
Clarke Street School.

Rankin, Dr. F. H.
Reynolds, G. B.
Reynolds, G. B. & Co,
Russell, Chas. H.
Richardson, J. D., Store,
Richardson, J. D., Residence.
Rives, Dr. Wm. C.
Rhinelander, F. W.
Robinson, Dr. Beverley.
Robbins, Henry
Robbins, G. E.
Rice, Henry H.
Reynolds & Dixon.
Rogers, Fairman, Residence.
Rogers, Fairman, Stable.
Rogers, Archibald.

Sayer, Julius.
Smith, Alfred.
Stanton & Squire.
Squire, Dr. A. F.
Stewart, A. & Co.
Stanhope, George.
Stedman, Wm. A.
Stevens, J. G.
Sherman, Chas. & Co.
Slocum & Black.
Stevens, Mrs. Paran.
Smith, G. & Co.
Smith, G deon.
Storer, Dr. H. R.
Swinburne, Peckham & Co.
Sanborn, John P., Office.
Sanborn, John P., Residence.
Seymore Mrs. C. M.
Sands, Mrs. A. L.
Stoddard, J. C. & Co.
Sherman, A. S.
State House.
Schwarz W. G.
Stevens, Mrs. J. A.
Sisson's Ice Cream.
Sears, Dr. S. H.
Seabury, T. M.
Swinburn, Wm. J.
Smith, E. C.
Spooner, E. G.
Stoddard, Wm. A.
Smith, John R.

Sanford, Milton H.
Spooner, Chas. E.
Sargent, Mrs. L. S.
Sticknor, Mrs. G.
Smith, Alfred & Sons.
Stedman, Marshall.
Shore Cottages.
Society for Prevention of Cruelty to Animals.

Tiffany, George.
Titus, A. C., Residence.
Titus, A. C., Store.
Tyler, Geo. F.
Tooker, G. M.
Tweedy, Edmond.
Tennant, D. B.
Thorn, W. K.
Thayer, Nathaniel, Jr.
Torrence, Daniel.
Taylor, Geo. H.
Tilley, H. H.
Tilton, Samuel.
Terry, Dr. R.
Tooker, Mrs. Mary.
Torpedo Station.
Thurber, Franklin.

U. S. Census Office.
U. S. Custom House.
U. S. Torpedo Station.

Van Emburgh & Atterbury.
Van Allen, General.
Vanderbilt, Cornelius.
Vanderbilt, Wm. K.

Waring. Geo. F. Jr., Residence.
Waring, Geo. E. Jr., Office.
Water Works Office.
Weaver, Chas. B.
Wilbur, Geo. V.
Willis, J. A.
Wilson, Ira E.
Whiting, Mrs. Sarah.
Weaver, Geo. H.
Ward, A J.
Whipple, John.
Washington, Mrs. S.
Western Union Telegraph Office.
Weaver, J. G. Jr.
Williamson, Wm. F.
Whitehouse, W. F.
Wer, Dr.
Watson, C.
Wright, H. Allen.
Wilson, Mrs. Wm. B.
Wickford Depot.
Winthrop, E. L.
Willing, E. S.
Wilbur Boarding House.
Wilson, Geo. H.
Ward, Remington.

Young Brothers.

✸The Newport Villa Owners' Guide✸

IS ON FILE AT THE FOLLOWING PLACES.

Albemarle Hotel,	New York City.	Ocean House,	Long Branch, N. J.
Astor House,	" "	Howland's Hotel,	" "
Brevoort House	" "	Mansion House,	" "
Buckingham Hotel.	" "	West End Hotel,	" "
Clarendon Hotel,	" "	Hotel Vendome,	Boston, Mass.
Everett House,	" "	Hotel Brunswick,	" "
Fifth Avenue Hotel,	" "	Parker House,	" "
Gilsey House,	" "	Young's Hotel,	" "
Glenham Hotel,	" "	Revere House,	" "
Grand Hotel,	" "	Tremont House,	" "
Grand Central Hotel.	" "	United States Hotel,	" "
Grammarcy Park Hotel,	" "	Grand Central Hotel,	Bar Harbor, Me.
Hoffman House,	" "	Rodick House,	" "
Grand Union Hotel,	" "	West End Hotel,	" "
Hotel Brunswick,	" "	Cooper House,	Cooperstown, N. Y.
Metropolitan Hotel,	" "	Hotel Fenimore,	" "
New York Hotel,	" "	Allyn House,	Hartford, Conn.
Park Avenue Hotel,	" "	United States Hotel,	" "
St. James Hotel,	" "	Fort George Hotel,	Lake George, N. Y.
St. Nicholas Hotel,	" "	Ft. Wm. Henry Hotel,	"
Sturtevant House,	" "	Nanapashemet,	Marblehead N'ck, Mass.
Leland's Hotel,	" "	Hotel Nantasket,	Nantasket Beach, "
Victoria Hotel.	" "	Hotel Pemberton,	" "
Vanderbilt Hotel,	" "	Atlantic House,	" "
Westminster Hotel.	" "	Rockland House,	" "
Windsor Hotel,	" "	Ocean House,	Nantucket, "
Ocean House,	Newport, R. I.	Mt. Hope House,	Narragansett Pier, R.I.
Aquidneck Hotel,	" "	The Wentworth,	Newcastle, N. H.
Perry House,	" "	Pequot House,	New London, Conn.
United States Hotel.	" "	Colonnade Hotel,	Philadelphia, Pa.
Hartman's,	" "	Continental Hotel,	" "
Brayton's,	" "	Girard House.	" "
Clarendon H'l,	Saratoga Springs, N. Y.	Maplewood Hall,	Pittsfield, Mass.
Congress Hall,	" "	Narragansett Hotel,	Providence, R. I.
Grand Union Hotel,	" "	Hotel Dorrance,	" "
United States Hotel,	" "	City Hotel,	" "
Windsor Hotel.	" "	Cozzens' Hotel,	West Point, N. Y.
Mountain House,	Catskill, N. Y.	West Point Hotel,	" "
Prospect Park Hotel,	" "		

BANKS.

Open Daily from 9 A.M. to 2 P.M.

AQUIDNECK NATIONAL BANK, 196 Thames street. Discount day, Monday.
FIRST NATIONAL BANK, 161 Thames street. Discount day, Friday.
MERCHANTS BANK, 153 Thames street. Discount day, Monday.
NATIONAL BANK OF RHODE ISLAND, of Newport, 219 Thames street. Discount day, Thursday.
NATIONAL EXCHANGE BANK, 30 Washington square. Discount day, Monday.
NEW ENGLAND COMMERCIAL BANK, 193 Thames street. Discount day, Tuesday.
NEWPORT NATIONAL BANK, 6 Washington square. Discount day, Tuesday.
UNION NATIONAL BANK, 178 Thames street. Discount day, Wednesday.

SAVINGS BANKS.

Open Daily from 9 A.M. to 2 P.M.

CODDINGTON SAVINGS BANK, 161 Thames street.
ISLAND SAVINGS BANK, 30 Washington square.
SAVINGS BANK OF NEWPORT, 194 Thames street.

TELEPHONE EXCHANGE.

NEWPORT AND SUBURBAN TELEPHONE EXCHANGE, Gas Company's Building, 177½ Thames street.

TELEGRAPH OFFICES.

MUTUAL UNION TELEGRAPH COMPANY, 175 Thames street (Branch, 4 Travers Block, Bellevue avenue.)
WESTERN UNION TELEGRAPH COMPANY, Thames street, near Franklin street (Branches at Ocean House and Perry House.)

EXPRESS OFFICES.

ADAMS EXPRESS COMPANY, Thames street, corner Pelham street.
NEWPORT TRANSFER COMPANY, Travers Block, Bellevue avenue.
NEW YORK AND BOSTON DESPATCH EXPRESS COMPANY, Gas Company's Building, 175 Thames street.

  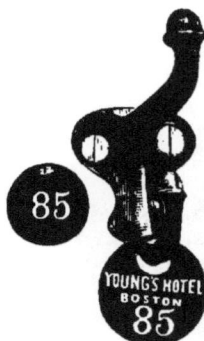

HOTELS.

Ambrose Dining Rooms	Thames Street.
Atwater House	Thames Street.
Aquidneck Hotel	Pelham, cor. Corne Street.
Bateman House	Bateman Point.
Bellevue Avenue Hotel . .	Bellevue Avenue, cor. Prospect Hill Street.
Brayton's	Pelham Street.
Cliff Avenue Hotel and Cottages	Cliff Road.
Cliff House	Near Annandale Road.
Germania Hotel	State, Foot of Downing Street.
Hartman's	Bellevue Avenue, near Kay Street.
Ocean House	Bellevue Avenue, cor. Bowery.
Park House	Washington Square.
Perry House . . .	Washington Square.
Pinard Cottages	Narragansett Avenue, near the Cliffs.
Sherman House	Thames Street.
United States Hotel	Thames, cor. Pelham Street.

Heights Above High Water Mark.

Quaker Hill.	280 00	Bellevue Ave., cor. Leroy Av.,		60 57
Miantonomi Hill,	157 77	" " Ruggles Av.,'		51 43
Highest point, Conanicut Island,	130 00	" " Marine Av.,		52 79
Telegraph Hill,	162 43	" " Yznaga Av.,		30 14
Thames Street, cor. Warner,	25 04	" " Ledge Road,		37 21
" " Long Wharf,	10 55	" " Perry Street,		69 47
" " Pelham,	15 71	" " Dixon Street,		66 39
" " Franklin,	14 34	" " Coggeshall		
" " Brenton Av.,	19 88	Av.,		24 48
Broadway, cor. State House,	26 92	Bellevue Ave., cor. Carroll Av.,		17 97
" " Mann Av.,	41 03	Fillmore Street, cor. Harrison Av.,		46 36
" " Bull Street,	33 49	King Street, cor. Harrison Av.,		58 56
" " Bedlow Av.,	94 06	Hill Side and Miantonomi Avs.,		78 97
" " Bliss Road,	78 44	Catherine Street, cor. R. I. Av.,		93 48
" " Miantonomi Av.,	123 32	Buena Vista Street, cor. R. I. Av.,		99 47
Washington Street, cor. Bridge,	10 60	Bath Road, cor. Annandale Road,		76 21
" " Battery,	21 94	" " Channing Av.,		36 98
Kay Street, cor. Rhode Island Av.,	49 84	" " R. I. Av.,		79 09
" " Gibbs Av.,	36 12	" " Gibbs Av.,		66 31
" " Mann Av.,	83 12	Spring Street, cor. Touro,		36 17
" " Touro Street,	86 26	" " Pelham,		41 94
Bellevue Ave., cor. Church,	91 71	" " Franklin,		38 21
" " Pelham,	91 31	" " Cannon,		37 20
" " Bowery,	77 66	" " Dearborn,		46 46
" " Bath Road,	84 37	Ocean Avenue, Carroll Avenue,		17 97
" " Narragansett Av.,	55 51			

H. H. DEAN. F. A. GLEASON. A. G. HUSSEY.

H. H. DEAN & CO.

COMMISSION MERCHANTS AND DEALERS IN

BUTTER, CHEESE, EGGS, BEANS, PORK AND LARD,

FANCY LUMP AND BOX BUTTER A SPECIALTY.

Buckwheat Flour. **Potatoes.**

Peas, (ALL KINDS.) **Poultry.**

Dried and Evaporated Apples. **Maple Sugar.**

All orders by mail promptly attended to.

37 JOHN STREET. - - - - BOSTON, MASS.

The Leading Business Houses of Newport.

Agricultural Implements.

Langley Job. T., 131 and 133 Thames.
Weaver George A., 19 Broadway.
Swinburne, Peckham & Co., 145 Thames.

Architects.

Fludder James, Fludder's block, Bellevue ave.
Ladd John G., Ladd Villa, Bath road.
Luce Clarence, Prospect Hill, corner Corne
Mason George C. & Son, Catherine, near Bellevue avenue.
Newton Dudley, Bellevue avenue, near Kay.

Art Furniture and Interior Decorator.

DIXWELL ARTHUR, 123 Bellevue avenue (see insert opp. p. 18)

Atomizers.

Essex Manufacturing Company, 230 Thames.

Auctioneers.

Baker A. Prescott, 12 Mount Vernon.
Bachellor Joshua B., 161 Spring.
Burlingham Thomas C., 23 Market square.
Carr Thomas T., 42 Bridge.
Crandall William H., 90 Broadway.
Dennis William E., 93 Thames.
Coggeshall Lawton, 12 Commercial wharf.
Freeborn Thomas W., 52 Broadway.
Helme Theodore R., 65 Spring.
Henderson Robert J., 83 Thames.
LAWTON GEORGE P., 23 Marlboro (see insert opp. p. 63).
Leonard, George P., Pond avenue, cor. Warner.
Peckham George E., 79 Thames.
Pray H. W., 42 Spring.
Stanhope Francis, 10 Broadway.
Ward A. Judson, Washington square.
Young Enoch G., Odd Fellows building, entrance on Charles street.

Baby Carriages.

LUTHER ALBERT W., *Daily News* block, 205 Thames (see p. 10)

Bakers.

ARNOLD JULIUS, 9 Broadway (see p. 34).
Davis Simeon, 205 Thames.
Franklin R. & W., Spring, corner Mary.
Lawton Charles L., 52 Bridge.

Bathing Houses.

Crosby Thomas, Easton's Beach.
Goffe Robert W., (blue houses,) Easton's Beach.

Bathing Goods and Suits.

Seabury J. E., 138 and 140 Thames.
SHERMAN WALTER, 140 Thames (see p. 16).
Taylor & Bennett, 119 Thames.

Bill Posters.

City Bill Posting Co., J. J. Flood, manager, Melville court, near Thames.

Blacksmiths.

Bates John, Kinsley's wharf.
Bliven Benjamin, Weaver ave., near Freebody.
Clark Peter F., Edward, corner Covell.
Clark Phineas C., near Long wharf.
Coggeshall Robert D., Commercial wharf
Cripps William W. L., 6 Sherman, near Spring.
Fayerweather Charles F. D., 7 West Broadway.
Goddard Charles S., 14 Farewell.

Holm A. M., Long wharf.
LEDDY JOHN E., 7 Farewell (see p. 40)
Lyons John, 14 Kinsley's wharf.
Quinn Martin, Bath road, near Freebody.
Scott Brothers, Spring, corner Sherman.
Shea Michael F., Burnside ave., near Davis ct.
Shea Patrick M., Clarendon court, near Bellevue avenue.
Smith William M., 27 West Broadway.
Tighe Thomas, Spring, near Perry.

Bleachers and Dyers.

French Augustus (hat and bonnet), 84 Br'dway.

Boat Builders.

Alger Nicholas B., foot of Long wharf.
Barlow Moses, 79 Long wharf.
Bliven Luke, Spring wharf.
Caswell Brothers, 66 Long wharf.
Fisher Clark D., 58 Long wharf.
Groff William B., 48 Long wharf.
Hart James N., 64 Long wharf.
Southwick Samuel S., 31 Long wharf.
Stoddard Thomas D., 68 Long wharf.

Book Binder and Blank Book Manufact'r.

Hammett Charles E. Jr., 124 Thames.

Booksellers and Stationers.

Clarke William P., 180 and 182 Thames.
Hammett Charles E. Jr., 124 Thames.
Norbury Levi, 224 Thames.
Jenkins William R., 8 Downing's block, Bellevue avenue.
ROGERS JOHN, 210 Thames (see inside back cover)
Tilley R. Hammett, 128 Thames.
TILLEY WM. LOVIE, 22 Washington square, (see p. 30).
Ward A. J., Odd Fellows b'ld'g, Washing'n sq.

Boot and Shoe Dealers.

Ailman Benjamin H. Jr., 112 Thames.
Alger Orin, 32 Broadway.
Brown John, 198 1-2 Thames.
Burdick Clark H. & Co., 267 Thames.
Holm Murdock S., Spring, near Mill.
Norman Thomas M. 2d, 142 Thames.
Palmer Benjamin F., 281 Thames.
Palmer George H., 103 Thames.
Popple J. M. & G. H., 72 Thames.
Seabury T. Mumford, 134 Thames.
Swan John M., 100 Thames.

Boot and Shoe Makers and Repairers.

Alger Orin, 32 Broadway.
Alger William, 6 Farewell.
Brown John, 198 1-2 Thames.
Coggeshall William, 1 Oak.
Dent Richard J., Young, near Thames.
Holm Murdock S., Spring, near Mill.
Joyce Walter Frank, rear 144 Thames.
Kane Joseph, Callendar avenue, near Davis ct.
Moorhead William T., 4 1-2 Mill.
Nealon James, Thames, near Dearborn.
Nelson Peter, Prospect Hill, near Bellevue ave.
Palmer Benjamin F., 281 Thames.
Palmer George H., 103 Thames.
Peckham Benjamin H., 45 Broadway.
Pedro Enos, 57 Spring.
Quire Peter, 15 Third.
Regan Thomas, 18 Young, near Spring.
Seabury T. Mumford, 134 Thames.
Silvia Frank, 4 Cannon.
Wilkey John H., 46 Thames.
Young Thomas E., 44 Poplar.

Bottlers.

Faerber Peter, Bull's wharf, rear 129 Thames.
Hazard James S., 14 Bath road.
Schade Adolph, Scott's wharf.
TRAEGER C. A., 31 Bath road.

Brewers.

Cooper William S., 3 and 5 Brewer.

Brick, Lime, and Cement.

Finch James B., Lopez wharf.
Swinburne, Peckham & Co., 145 Thames.

Brokers.

Bull Henry, Jr., 129 Thames (stock and bonds).
Crocker Edward A. (real estate and insurance), Bellevue avenue, near Kay.
FLAGG GEORGE W., 175 Thames
Howard J. Neilson & Co. (real estate), Bellevue avenue, near Casino.
PORTER FRANK B. & CO. (real estate), Bellevue avenue, near Kay.
Read Oliver (stock and bonds), 161 Thames.
Van Amburgh & Atterbury, Ocean House.
Watson Daniel (real estate), 165 Thames.
Wilbur George V., Bellevue avenue, near Kay

Brushes.

Caswell, Massey & Co., 167 Thames, and 6 Casino building, Bellevue avenue.
Weaver George A., 19 Broadway.

Building Materials.

Finch James B., Lopez wharf.
Hammett Albert, 201 Thames.
Langley Job T., 131 and 133 Thames.
Sayer Joshua, Sayer's wharf.
Swinburne, Peckham & Co., 145 Thames.

Butchers.

Smith G. & Co. (Chicago dressed beef at wholesale), Long wharf, rear Old Colony depot.

Cabinet Makers.

Barber Charles P., 4 and 6 Market square.
Vernon George E., 34 John.

Canned Goods.

Bryer Peleg, 21 and 23 Broadway.
Carry Brothers, 187 and 189 Thames.
Crosby John H. Jr., Bellevue ave., cor. Levin.
DeBlois John B., 15 Broadway.
Dennis William E., 93 Thames.
Sayer Julius, 207 Thames.
Scott H. D., 223 Thames.
Stanhope George, 201 Thames.
Williamson William F., 204 Thames.

Carpenters and Builders.

Albro D. P., Third, corner Cherry.
Anderson & McLean, Cotton's ct., n. Thames.
Barker Nathan, Elizabeth, corner Centre.
Bowen George W., over 23 Long wharf.
Brotherson Moses, 60 Spring.
Burdick Charles H., 11 Howard, near Spring.
Case P. G. & Co., Sherman's whf., n Thames.
Coffin William B., Kilburn court, n Broadway.
Cranston William S., Brown & Howard's whf.
Easton Benjamin, Gould, near Broadway.
Fisher Clark D., 58 Long wharf.
Hamilton William, 38 Bridge.
Hammett John R., William, near Spring.
Johnston J. D., 29 Mill.
Kaull H. Augustus, 6 Cross.
McCormick Michael, Dearborn, near Spring.
McIntosh Alexander, 29 Bath road.
Morgan Frank, Caleb Earl, near W. Broadway.
Peabody John, Sunshine court, e. Gladding et.
Peckham Cyrus H., Perry, near Grant court.
Peckham William P., Kilburn court.
Potter James C., Gould, near Broadway.
Tanner Benjamin F., 6 Commercial wharf.
Tripp William E., West, near Pope.
Wilson George H., Cottage, corner Redwood.

Carpet Dealers.

Cozzens William C. & Co., 74 1-2 Thames.
Hammett William H., 174 Thames.
Lawton Edward W., 126 Thames.

Carriage Manufacturers.

BREWSTER J. B. & CO., Bellevue avenue, cor. Downing
Burdick Thomas S., 16 Farewell.
Cripps William W. L., Sherman, near Spring.
Holm A. M., Long wharf.
Scott Brothers, Spring, corner Sherman
Seatle Charles H., Weaver ave., n. Freebody.
Smith William M., 27 West Broadway.
Stevens Achilles, 24 Spring, corner Barney.
Wilson James H., 9 1-2 Mann ave., near Kay.
Wood Andrew T, 6 Sherman, near Spring.

Carriage and Coach Painters.

BURDICK ARNOLD L., 382 and 384 Spring, and Weaver avenue, n. Ocean House (see p. 28)
Holm A. M., Long wharf.
Lauders William B, 6 Sherman, near Spring.
Marchington William, Burnside avenue, near Davis court.
Sullivan Cornelius S., over 14 Farewell.

Carriage Repositories.

BURDICK ARNOLD L., Weaver avenue, rear Ocean House (see p. 28).
LAWTON GEO. P., 23 to 33 Marlboro.

Carriage and Coach Trimmer.

Wetherell John H., 6 Sherman, near Spring.

Caterers.

Gilmore Spencer H., Bellevue ave., cor. John.
Hertgen Carl, 72 Spring, and Easton's Beach.

Chemists.

(See also Druggists.)

Caswell, Massey & Co., 167 Thames, and 6 Casino building, Bellevue avenue.
Downing B. F. Jr., 36 and 38 Broadway.
Groff John E., 210 Thames.

Cigar and Tobacco Dealers.

Bickerton Charles, 2 Mill.
Bryer John H., 192 Thames.
Centennial Tea Company, 88 Thames.
Goffe Ernest, 59 Thames.
GORTON EVERETT L., 278 Thames (see p. 18).
Hidler J. D., 203 Thames.
Holmes James H., 3 Long wharf.
Lewis & Tilley, 156 Thames.
Marchington Matthew, 211 Thames.
Norbury Levi, 224 Thames.
Richardson John D., 212 Thames.
Rutherford William T., 179 Thames.
TILLEY WILLIAM LOVIE, 22 Washington sq.
Tripp John T., 24 Broadway.
Williamson William F., 204 Thames,

Civil Engineer and Surveyor.

JUDSON J. A. CAPT., Fludder's block, Bellevue avenue, near Kay (see p. 24).

Clothing Dealers.

Callaghan Mary A. Mrs. (second hand), 70 Spring.
Cozzens John H. & Son, 152 Thames
Goffe Augustus, Gas Co.'s building, 77 Thames
Gould & Son, 70 Thames
Munro George C., 158 Thames
NEWPORT ONE PRICE CLOTHING STORE, 211 Thames
New York One Price Clothing House, Thames street
Seabury J. E., 138 and 140 Thames
Taylor & Bennett, 119 Thames

Coach Builders.

BREWSTER J. B. & CO., Bellevue avenue, cor.
Downing

Coal and Wood Dealers.

Bowen George, Heirs of, James C. Swan, agt.,
8 Bowen's wharf
Brown & Howard, Brown & Howard's wharf
Perry Brothers, Perry Brothers' wharf
Pinniger & Manchester, Perry Mill wharf
Reynolds Gardiner B. & Co., Langley's and
Sherman's wharves, also opposite post-office
Swinburne William J., 107 Thames

Coffins, Caskets, Etc.

Langley John S., 10 Franklin

Collars, Gloves, and Hosiery.

Atwater John C., 198 Thames
Gould & Son, 70 Thames
O'Neill Thomas J., 162 Thames
Seabury J. E., 138 and 140 Thames
Tayler & Bennett, 119 Thames

Commissioners for other States.

Brinley Francis (New York and Massachusetts),
127 Thames
Honey Samuel R. (New York), 127 Thames

Confectioners.

Centennial Tea Company, 88 Thames
Chadwick James H., 247 Thames
Dorsey Jacob, Warner, near Burnside avenue
Frasch Charles F., 102 Thames
Hammond Newton, Horgan's block, Bellevue
avenue, opp. John
Hertgen Carl, 72 Spring, and Easton's Beach
Jones Joseph T., 23 Thames
Kuhn William F., 99 Spring, corner Franklin
Peters Anton, 30 Broadway
Muenchinger & Sons, 150 Thames, and Bellevue
avenue, corner Mill
SIMPSON JOSEPH H., Bellevue ave. (see p. 6).
Sisson William, Bellevue ave., n. Clarendon ct.
Taylor George H., Spring, corner Touro
Washington George Mrs., 1 Downing's block,
Bellevue avenue
Westall Simeon, 24 1-2 Elm

Contractors.

Anderson & McLean, Cotton's ct., n. Thames
Barker Nathan, Centre, corner Elizabeth
Bowen George W., over 25 Long wharf
Burdick Charles H., 11 Howard, near Spring
Fludder William & Co. (masons), Bellevue ave-
nue, corner Catherine
Hamilton William, 38 Bridge
Underwood William J. (mason), Weaver ave-
nue, near Freebody

Cotton Goods Manufacturers.

Perry Mill Co. (print cloths), S. C. Bailey, treas-
urer and agent, corner Perry Mill wharf
Richmond Manufacturing Co. (print cloths),
John Congdon, superintendent, Thames, cor.
Aquidneck Mill wharf

Cracker Dealers.

R. & W. Franklin, Spring, corner Mary

Crockery, China, and Glass Ware.

Allan Erastus P., 63 and 65 Thames
Brown James B., 122 Thames
Centennial Tea Company, 88 Thames
LANDERS A. C., 165 Thames (see p. 30)
LUTHER ALBERT W., Daily News block, 135
Thames (see advt. p. 10)
Marden James F., 4 and 5 Cottrell's block,
Thames
Parker William, 256 Thames
Williams C. S., 28 Broadway

Dentists.

Angell Avery F., 165 Thames.
Brackett Charles A., 64 Touro, cor. Mt. Vernon.
Bradley Thomas, 72 Touro, near Kay.
Greene Samuel E., 124 Thames.
Smith J. William, 64 Touro, cor. Mt. Vernon.
Smith William H., 45 Pelham.
Stoddard William C., 5 Touro.

"Domestic" Paper Fashions.

SHERMAN WALTER, 140 Thames (see p. 16).

Doors, Sashes, and Blinds.

Bosworth Smith & Co., West Broadway, corner
Green lane
Swinburne, Peckham & Co., 145 Thames

Drain and Sewer Pipe.

Finch James B., Lopez wharf
Sayer Joshua, Sayer's wharf

Druggists.

Allan Wm. S. N., 18 Washington square
Caswell, Hazard & Co., 132 Thames
Caswell, Massey & Co., 167 Thames, and 6 Cas-
ino building, Bellevue ave.
Cotton William H., 146 Thames
Downing B. F. Jr., 36 and 38 Broadway
Groff John E., 210 Thames
Irish Ephraim B. (botanic), 44 Thames
Taylor James H, 104 Thames

Dry Goods.

Barkinshaw & Marvel, 278 and 280 Thames, cor.
Howard
Carr G. W. & T. T., 46 Bridge
Cremin Mary E. Mrs., 315 Thames
Denman John B. F., 121 Thames
Ginsburg Louis, 64 Thames
Greene A. C., 44 Broadway
Hammett James H., 98 Broadway
Hayes Thomas Mrs., Thames, cor. Wellington
avenue
King & McLeod, 74 Thames
Lawton Edward W., 126 Thames
Levi Isaac, 279 Thames, near Young
Martin John, Thames, near Lee avenue
Rosen Maurice, 320 Thames
Sayer A. C. Miss (worsteds and embroideries),
116 Thames
Sherman Albert, 259 Thames
SHERMAN WALTER, 140 Thames (see p. 16)
Sherman William & Co., 67 and 69 Thames
Sherman William B. Jr., 108 Thames
Stewart Sumner M., 260 Thames
Turner H. E. Jr. & Bro., 154 Thames
Waite Freeborn S., 213 Thames

Electric Batteries and Exploders.

Hill M. W. & Co., Commercial wharf

Electricians.

COZZENS & BULL, Gas Light Co.'s building,
177 1-2 Thames
Wilks Frank H., 2 Scott's wharf

Emigration Agents.

Brown John, 198 1-2 Thames
Denniston George, 26 Kinsley's wharf

Expresses and Expressmen.

Adams Express Co. (all parts of the country),
Charles H. White, agent, 186 Thames
Eddy Michael (local), 36 Division
NEWPORT TRANSFER CO., B. J. Burton, agt.,
4 Travers block, Bellevue avenue, and 175
Thames (see p. 20)
NEW YORK AND BOSTON DESPATCH EX-
PRESS CO. (to all parts of the country), J. L.
Greene, agent, 175 Thames (see p. 20)
Peckham William G. (local), 39 Bridge

Expresses and Expressmen,—continued.

Potter Thomas J., Hall avenue, near Gibbs
Tefft Stephen N., Gladding ct, near Sunshine ct
West Charles H., (local) 87 Thames
Wilcox Albert G. Jr., (local,) Connection, near Thames
Willis James A., (local,) 201 Thames

Fancy Goods.

Allen Erastus P., 63 and 65 Thames
Elias Jonas, 40 Levin
Harris Ulysses G., 249 Thames   [ave
Keogh M E. Miss, 6 Downing's block, Bellevue
LANDERS ALBERT C., 165 Thames, (see p. 30)
Lawton Edward W., 126 Thames
LUTHER A. W., Daily News block, 135 Thames
Morimura Bros. (Japanese goods), 6 Travers block, Bellevue avenue
Norbury Levi, 224 Thames
Schmidt Anthony, 5 Travers blk., Bellevue ave.
SHERMAN WALTER, 140 Thames (see p. 16)
Simpson John, Bellevue ave., cor. William
Tilley R. Hammett, 128 Thames
Turner H. E. Jr. & Bro., 154 Thames
Weaver L. P. Miss, 24 Washington square

Fancy Groceries and Tea Dealers.

Bryer Peleg, 21 and 23 Broadway
Centennial Tea Co., Ira E. Wilson, proprietor, 88 Thames

Fertilizers.

Peckham John H. (Stockbridge manures), 72 and 72 1-2 Broadway
Weaver Geo. A. (all kinds), 19 Broadway

Fish and Oyster Markets.

Albro Samuel, 159 Thames
Carry Brothers, 187 and 189 Thames
Congdon John A., Commercial wharf
Griffith Edward, 51 Long wharf
Kaull George C. Jr., 22 Broadway
Lancaster J. P., 86 Broadway
Lawton W. H. H., 43 Long wharf
Lee Brothers, 179 Thames
Lee Peter J., foot Scott's wharf
Lee Thomas J., 224 1-2 Thames
Lloyd George L., 22 Ferry wharf
Smith Edward C., 307 Thames
Thompson Noah, Kinsley's wharf

Florists.

Brandt Arend, Gibbs, near Farewell
Butler Henry, Casino Block
Fadden Frederick W., Bellevue avenue, near Bath road
Findlay William, North Kay, near Bliss road
Geraghty Thomas H., Cottage place, n. Beach
Greer James, Tompkins court, corner Fillmore, rear Catherine
Hardwick George, Coggeshall ave., near Bancroft avenue
Hass Henry J., Vernon ave., near Broadway
Hodgson James M., Bellevue avenue, corner Leroy avenue
Jurgens Carl H., 13 Mill
Klunder Charles F., 8 Travers block, Bellevue avenue
Maher William H., Coggeshall avenue, opposite Wheatland avenue
McLeish James, Wilbar, near Wellington ave.
Reynolds Richard, Warner, cor. Burnside ave.
Smith Samuel, Bellevue avenue, opp. Prospect Hill
Thurston Benjamin M., Broadway, near Thurston avenue
Wilson Fletcher, Wilbar, near Wellington ave.
Wilson Robert, Broadway, near Malbone ave.

Flour and Grain.

Briggs & Co., 38 1-2 Thames
Mason John B., 243 Thames
Murray Charles S., 298 Thames
Peckham John H., 72 and 72 1-2 Broadway

Pritchard N. C., 107 Thames
Sayer Joshua, Sayer's wharf
Spooner Charles E., Commercial wharf
Stevens Thomas, 3 Market square

Fruit and Nuts.

Brown James A., 16 Market square
CALDWELL & BACON, Bellevue, corner Bath road (see p. 56)
Carry Brothers, 187 and 189 Thames
Centennial Tea Company, 88 Thames
Clark Thomas C., 32 Washington square
Crosby John H. Jr., Bellevue ave., cor. Levin.
DeBlois John B., 15 Broadway
Grenson Lawrence M., 308 Thames
Hazard George M., 2 Broadway
Johnson Obadiah K., 155 Thames
Lee Brothers, 179 Thames
Lewis & Tilley, 156 Thames
Pitman John, 19 Thames, corner Bridge
Potter Stephen A., 42 Broadway
Smith Edward C., 307 Thames
Stanhope George, 201 Thames
Taylor George H., Spring, cor. Touro
Thurston James T., 228 Thames
Williams Charles S., 28 Broadway
Williamson William F., 204 Thames
Wilson Frank M., 79 Thames

Furnaces and Ranges.

Marden James F., 4 and 5 Cottrell's block, Thames
Southwick J. M. K., 117 Thames
Walsh Brothers, 11 Market square.

Furniture Dealers and Cabinet Makers.

Bryer Stafford, 90 Thames
Chadwick John (antique and art furniture) Berkeley building, Bellevue avenue
Cottrell M., 2 and 3 Cottrell's block, 222 Thames
DIXWELL ARTHUR, 123 Bellevue avenue (see insert, opp. p. 18)
Flannagan Patrick (new and second-hand), 258 Thames
Hazard J. L. & G. A., 23 Church
Krafft Herman, Franklin, corner Spring
Langley John S., 10 Franklin
Leary Annie B. Mrs. (second-hand), 24 West Broadway
Markward & Staab, 2 Travers block, Bellevue avenue
Marsh E. P., 87 Thames
Smith George B., 40 Broadway
Stedman Stephen M., 66 Spring
Sypher & Co. (antique), 5 Casino building, Bellevue avenue
Titus Augustin C., 235 Thames

Games.

LANDERS A. C., 165 Thames (see p. 30)
LUTHER A. W., Daily News block, 205 Thames (see p. 10)

Gas Fittings and Fixtures.

Barker Brothers, 5 Market square
Conroy Philip F. & Co., 317 Thames
Grenson Clarence, 67 Spring
McAdam & Openshaw, 6 Mill
Newport Gas Light Company, 179 Thames

Gas Stoves.

Newport Gas Light Company, 179 Thames

Gents' Furnishing Goods.

Atwater John C., 198 Thames
Gould & Son, 70 Thames
Greene the Hatter, Thames street
Hammett William H., 174 Thames
O'Neill T. J., 162 Thames
Riley Joseph H., 114 Thames
Seabury J. E., 138 and 140 Thames
Simpson John, Bellevue ave., cor. William
Taylor & Bennett, 119 Thames

Glass.

Gilman Edward V., 23 Long wharf
Stoddard John C. & Co., 9 Long wharf

Granite Workers and Dealers.

Cottrell J. B., Warner, near Callender avenue
McGowan P., Sherman's wharf
Stevens' P. Sons, 11 Thames

Grist Mills.

Spooner Charles E., Commercial wharf

Grocers.

Aldred Abraham W., 272 Thames
Allan, William, Stone, corner Spring
Barber Charles P., 4 and 6 Market square
Barker A. A., 114 Broadway
Barker Henry, 17 Second
Barker Robert S., 163 Thames
Barker William A. & Co., 66 Bridge
Brierly James, 266 Thames, corner Young
Bryer Peleg, 21 and 23 Broadway
Buckley Patrick, Callendar ave., n. Davis st.
Burdick J. Truman, 269 and 271 Thames
Birkinshaw & Marvel, 278 and 280 Thames, cor. Howard
Carr Thomas T., 42 Bridge
Carroll John F., Bowery, near Middleton ave.
Clark Thomas C., 32 Washington square
Coen Joseph V., 76 Long wharf
Cornell & Son, 25 and 27 Broadway
Cottrell James B., Thames, corner Pope
Crosby John H. Jr., Bellevue ave., cor. Levin
Curtis John, 40 Bridge
DeBlois John B., 15 Broadway
DeFray Manuel Mrs., 17 Chesnut, cor. Third
Dennis William E., 93 Thames
Denniston George, 26 Kinsley's wharf
Driscoll Michael, Thames, near Dearborn
Eddy James A., Thames, corner Cannon
Halpine Patrick H., 3 Spruce
Hamilton Robert F., Third, corner Poplar
Hayes Thomas, Thames, cor. Wellington ave.
Hazard Silas H., Spring, corner Church
Horgan James D., 48 West Broadway
Horgan James J., Callendar ave., e. Davis st.
Horgan Patrick H., 30 West Broadway
Hughes Edward F., 22 William
Kenney Martin, Lee avenue, corner Spring
Lake Thomas J., Spruce, near Warner
Lawton Charles L., 32 Bridge
Lynch Mary A. Mrs., foot of Market square
Maher John, Thames, cor. Coddington wharf
Martin John, Thames, corner Holland
Martin John, Thames, corner Lee avenue
McMahon & Dugan, West Broadway, cor. Burnside avenue
Mumford William E., 3 DeBlois block, Bellevue avenue
O'Connell Thomas, Clinton avenue, c. Warner
O'Keeffe Patrick, 7 Dixon's lane
O'Leary James, Thames, corner Sharon court
Peckham John H., 72 and 72 1-2 Broadway
Peckham & Manchester, 62 Broadway
Perkins George W., 46 Spring
Pike Joseph B., 12 1-2 Third
Reagan Michael O., 383 Thames
Sayer Joshua, Sayer's wharf
Sayer Julius, 207 Thames
Scott H. D., 223 Thames
Shea John J., Callender ave., n. Davis court
Sheehan D. W., 19 Kinsley's wharf
Sherman C. & Co. (wholesale and retail), 8 and 10 Market square
Simmons Lewis L., 21 Spring
Stanhope George, 201 Thames
Stevens B. Hammett, 26 1-2 Thames
Stevens Philip, 22 and 24 Thames
Sullivan John & Coggeshall O., 357 Thames, cor. Dixon's lane
Sullivan Timothy C., Thames, e. South Baptist
Sullivan Timothy W., 326 Thames
Sutherland Andrew, Thames, corner Pope
Taylor Edward E., 346 Thames corner Underwood court

Thurston Ruth E. Mrs., 144 Spring
Walsh Richard J., Gould, corner Warner
Weaver James L., 6 1-2 Willow
Williams Charles S., 28 Broadway
Wilson Ira E., 88 Thames
Young Brothers, 7 and 9 Touro

Hairdressers.

Allen William, 79 Thames
Anderson Gorton, 119 1-2 Thames
Beams James, 284 Thames
Bowman Charles, Thames, cor. South Baptist
Brickelmaier Edmund, 165 Thames
Danahy Cornelius V., 147 Thames
Dawley Theodore B., 191 Thames
Douglas David, 4 Cannon
Dugan John M., 119 1-2 Thames
Gladding James M., 24 Broadway, at John T. Tripp's
Gooden William H., 20 West Broadway
Holmes James H., 3 Long wharf
Jackson William, 62 Bridge
Nason George E., 197 Thames
Terner Charles, 203 Thames
Washington George, 2 Downing's block, Bellevue avenue
Watson, William H., 32 Marlborough
Williams Fred E., 3 Morgan's bl'k, Bellevue ave.
Williams Thomas G., 44 Levin
Young Enoch G., Odd Fellows building, entrance on Charles street

Hardware and Cutlery.

Hammett Albert, 231 Thames
Langley Job T., 131 and 135 Thames
Southwick J. M. K. (marine hardware), 117 Thames
Swinburne, Peckham & Co., 145 Thames
Weaver George A., 19 Broadway

Harnesses, Saddle Makers and Horse Clothing.

BIESEL HENRY, People's Library building, 176 Thames (see p. 12)
Buck George C. & Co., 7 Downing's block, Bellevue avenue
Easterbrooks James A., 16 Touro
Gallagher Francis A., 3 Farewell
Gratrix George, 18 Broadway, and 10 Travers block, Bellevue avenue
Lawton George, 36 Marlborough
McCARTY BROS., Cottrell's block (see insert), opp. p. 62)
Tuell Arthur R., rear Ocean House

Hats and Caps.

Atwater John C., 198 Thames
Gladding O. H. P., 85 Thames
Greene Fred W., 72 1-2 Thames
Norbury Levi, 224 Thames
O'Neill T. J., 162 Thames
Seabury J. E., 138 and 140 Thames
Yates W. & A. (silk hat manufacturers), Spring, near Mill

Hay, Straw, and Feed.

Mason John B., 243 Thames
Murray Charles S., 298 Thames
Sayer Joshua, sayer's wharf
Spooner Charles E., Commercial wharf
Stevens Thomas, 3 Market square

Hides and Wool Skins.

Smith G. & Co., Long whf., n. Old Colony depot

Horse Shoers.

Clark Peter F., Edward, corner Covell
Coggeshall Robert D., Commercial wharf
Fayerweather Charles F. D., 7 West Broadway
LEDDY JOHN E., 7 Farewell (see p. 40)
Lineham George N., 17, 19 and 21 W. Broadway
Lyons John, 14 Kinsley's wharf
Murphy John A., 30 Marlborough, corner West Broadway

Horse Shoers—Continued.

Quinn Martin, Bath road, opp. Freebody
Shea Patrick M., Clarendon court, near Bellevue avenue
Tighe Thomas, Spring, near Perry

House Furnishing Goods.

Brown James B., agent, 122 Thames
Bryer Stafford, 90 Thames
Cottrell M., 2 and 3 Cottrell's block, 222 Thames
Covell William K. Jr., 163 Thames
Langley & Sharpe, 195 Thames
Marden James F., 4 and 5 Cottrell's block
Marsh E. P., 87 Thames
Southwick J. M. K., 117 Thames
Walsh Brothers, 11 Market square

Ice Cream Saloons.

Hammond Newton, Bellevue av. opp. John
HOUGHTON GEO. E., 184 Thames (see p. 18)
Frasch Charles F., 102 Thames

Ice Dealers.

Citizens' Ice Co., William Albro, proprietor, Long wharf
Newport Ice Co., John H. Greene, superintendent, Commercial

Insurance Offices.

Ball Henry, Jr., 129 Thames
Crocker Edward A., Bellevue ave. near Kay
Davis Lucius D., 157 Thames
Howard J. N. & Co., Bellevue av. near Casino
Langley Job T., 131 and 133 Thames
Marsh Benjamin, 2d. 5 Touro
Sherman A. S., office Merchants Bank, 153 Thames
Ward Henry N., State House

Japanese Goods.

Morimura Brothers, 6 Travers block, Bellevue avenue.

Jewelry, Watches, &c.

Blain, Edwin C., 164 Thames
Cummings Daniel L., 80 Thames
Denham D. C., 190 Thames
Farrow W. Milton, 66 Thames
Heath H. A. & Co., 96 Thames
Hermann George O., 149 Thames
Howard & Co., 8 Casino Building, Bellevue av.
Pitman William R., 35 Broadway
Pray H. W., 42 Spring
SPINGLER ALBERT G., 13 Franklin (see p. 26)

Lamps and Oils.

Centennial Tea Co., 88 Thames
LANDERS A. C., 165 Thames (see p. 30)
LUTHER A. W., Daily News block, 205 Thames see p. 10)

Landscape Gardeners.

Butler Henry, Casino block
Greer James, Tompkins court, cor. Fillmore ct.
Hodgson James M., Bellevue, cor. Leroy ave.
Maher William H., Coggeshall avenue, opposite Wheatland avenue

Laundries.

Bonetat Auguste (French), Southmayd, near Farewell
Moore James M., Long wharf, near Thames
Newport Steam Laundry, George P. Leonard, proprietor, Pond avenue, corner Warner
Toogood Mrs. Belinda, 13 Bath road
Young Lee (Chinese), 4 1-2 Prospect Hill

Lawn Mowers, Plows, and Pumps.

Weaver George A., 23 Broadway

Lawyers.

Baker Darius, 139 Thames
Galvin Patrick J., over 181 Thames
Gilpin William, 185 Thames
Honey Samuel B., 127 Thames
Lee Christopher M., over 131 and 133 Thames
Peckham F. B. Jr., over 131 and 133 Thames
Sheffield William P., 155 Thames
Sheffield William P. Jr., 155 Thames
Van Zandt Charles C., 127 Thames

Libraries.

People's Library, 178 Thames
Redwood Library and Athenaeum, Bellevue avenue, corner Redwood

Lime, Plaster, and Cement.

Finch James B., Lopez wharf
Swinburne, Peckham & Co., 145 Thames

Locksmiths and Bell Hangers.

Gladding Christopher, 69 Spring
Glynn John, room 19 Travers block, Bellevue avenue

Lumber Dealers.

Bosworth, Smith & Co., West Broadway, corner Green lane
Finch James B., Lopez wharf
Greene A. G. & Son, 13 Church
Hammett Albert, 231 Thames
Sayer Joshua (hard wood), Sayer's wharf
Swinburne, Peckham & Co., 145 Thames

Machinists and Machinery Manufacturers.

Weaver George A., 19 Broadway
Wilks Frank H. (also electrician), 2 Scott's wharf

Marble Workers.

Cottrell James B., Warner, near Calendar ave.
McGowan P., Sherman's wharf
Stevens' P. Sons, 11 Thames

Market Gardeners.

Dodge Edward T., Hall avenue, near Warner
Dodge William R., Warner, opposite Newport avenue

Masons.

Fludder William & Co., Bellevue avenue, corner Catherine
Freeborn John, 4 Third
Knowe Peter, 11 Gould near Warner
McCormick John, Dearborn, near Spring
Underwood William J., Weaver avenue, near Freebody

Merchant Tailors.

Alderson John, Whitehall block, Bellevue ave.
Dale Edward, 233 Thames
Gould & Son, 70 Thames
Lambert Desire J., 10 Pelham
Langley William C., 104 and 106 Thames
O'CONNOR JOHN, 315 Thames (see p. 24)
Otto Edward, 1 Cottrell's block, 222 Thames
Riley Henry C., 114 Thames
Swan Edward P., 168 Thames

Milliners and Millinery Goods.

Boyle J. E. Mrs., Touro, corner Spring
Carney Ellen M. Miss, 1 Broadway
Coffin A. L. Mrs., 1 Franklin
Cottrell Mary F. Miss, 7 Franklin
Dawley Florence N. Miss, 10 Brewer
DONOVAN C. MRS., Casino building, Bellevue avenue (see insert, opp. p. 36)
Elias L. C. Miss, 49 Levin
Guerin Albert, 2 Abrahams bl'k, Bellevue ave.
Haddock Helen E. Miss, 38 and 40 Washington square

Milliners and Millinery Goods—Continued.

Harris Ulysses G., 249 Thames
Hood Rebecca Miss, 1 Abrahams block, Bellevue avenue
Langley & Saunders, 120 Thames
Southwick W. D. Mrs., 55 Thames
Spooner Hannah B. Miss, 5 Bull
Wheeler Hannah M. Mrs., 6 Fair

Music and Musical Instruments.

ROGERS JOHN, 210 Thames (see inside back cover)

Oil Stoves.

Covell William K., Jr., agent Florence Oil Stoves, 95 and 97 Thames
Marden James F., 4 and 5 Cottrell's block, 222 Thames
Southwick J. M. K., 117 Thames

Optician.

Blain Edwin C., 164 Thames

Painters—House, Sign, Carriage, &c.

Allen John B (house and sign), 6 Broadway
Almy Abram (house), 5 Oak
Austin John R. (house), 7 Mill
Austin William M. 119 Spring
Barker George C. & Son, 41 Spring
Brett John J. (house), 12 Extension, near Thames
BURDICK ARNOLD L., carriage painter, Weaver avenue, near Ocean House, and house and sign painter, 382 and 384 Spring (see p. 28)
Burdick Henry C. (house and sign), 5 Commercial wharf
Cooper James C., Jr. (house, sign and ornamental), 3 Mill
Crabb Geo. W., 36 and 38 Broadway
Gay Bradford (house) Commercial wharf
Gilman Edward V., 23 Long wharf
Green William H. (house), 143 Thames
Holm A. M. (carriage), Long wharf
Hudson Robert, 1 West
Landers William R. carriage and ornamental, 6 Sherman, near Spring
Marchington Wm. (carriage), Burnside avenue, near Davis court
Mayer Joseph (fresco), 11 Cross.
Newell John P., 254 Thames.
Smith John B. F. (house and sign), 12 John.
Stoddard John C. & Co. (house and sign), 9 Long wharf
Sullivan Cornelius S., over 14 Farewell.
Taylor & Howard (carriage and sign), 24 Spring, corner Barney.
White Charles E. (house and sign), 343 Thames
Wiles Frederick T (house), Prospect Hill, near Bellevue avenue

Painters—Portrait and Landscape.

Hayman William E. B. (fresco), 2 Elm
Newell John P. (also marine), 254 Thames
Stuart Jane Miss, 30 Mill

Paints, Oils, Glass, Etc.

Allen John B., 6 Broadway
Almy Abram, 5 Oak
Bowen George W., over 23 Long wharf
BURDICK ARNOLD L., Weaver avenue, near Ocean House, and 382 & 384 Spring, (see p. 28)
Cooper James C, Jr., 3 Mill
Gilman Edward V., 23 Long wharf
Green W. H., 143 Thames
Langley Job T., 131 and 133 Thames
Sayer Joshua, Sayer's wharf
Stoddard John C. & Co., 9 Long wharf
Weaver George A., 19 Broadway
White Charles E., 343 Thames

Paper Hangers.

Allen John B., 6 Broadway
Almy Abram, 5 Oak

Brett John J., 12 Extension, near Thames
Burdick Henry C., 5 Commercial wharf
Cooper James C., Jr., 3 Mill
Crandall Charles, 10 Green
Palmer Benjamin G., 25 Church
Stoddard John C. & Co., 9 Long wharf
White Charles E., 343 Thames

Patent Medicines.

Caswell, Massey & Co., 167 Thames, and 6 Casino building, Bellevue avenue
Downing B. F., Jr., 36 and 38 Broadway
Groff John E., 210 Thames
Taylor James H., 194 Thames

Periodical and News Dealers.

Clarke William P., 180 and 182 Thames
Gash Thomas, Thames, near Lee's wharf
Goffe Ernest, 59 Thames
Jenkins W. R., 8 Downing's bl'k, Bellevue ave
Norbury Levi, 224 Thames
Tilley R. Hammett, 128 Thames
TILLEY WILLIAM LOVIE, 22 Washington sq. (see p. 30)

Photographers.

Child Robert H., 160 Thames
Leavitt Aaron L., 127 Thames
LUDOVICI JULIUS, Bellevue ave., near Mill (see p. 18)
NOTMAN PHOTOGRAPHIC CO., Bellevue avenue, opp. Redwood (see p. 32)

Physicians.

Barker Christopher F., 20 Division
Birckhead William H., 29 Touro, corner High
Chace N. R., 33 Touro, near School
Curley John P., Bath road, near Bellevue ave.
Engs George, Fludder's block, Bellevue ave.
Fisher Charles L., 51 Church
Francis Samuel W., Fludder's block, Bellevue
Greene William B., 63 Washington
Hurley John F., Dearborn, near Spring
McKim W. D., 29 Touro
News Annie Miss, 29 Touro
Odell George M., 4 Kay, near Touro
Powell Stephen C., Beach, cor. Cottage place
Rankin Francis B., 9 Catherine
Rice Richard B., 48 Farewell
Sears Stephen H., Touro, corner High
Stanton & Squire, 6 Pelham
Turner Henry E., 6 School

• Pianos and Organs.

ROGERS JOHN, 210 Thames (see inside back cover)
Swan Richard, 172 Thames

Piano Tuner.

Vars John, 5 Sherman

Pleasure Boats.

Bliven Luke Jr., Spring wharf, near Thames
Martland Thomas, 27 Kinsley's wharf
Thompson Noah, Kinsley's wharf

Plumbers and Coppersmiths.

Conroy Philip F. & Co., 171 Thames
Cremin & Butler, 14 Franklin
Greason Clarence, 67 Spring
Lyon Joseph W., 236 Thames
McAdam and Openshaw, 6 Mill
Oman Robert L., 31 Broadway

Printers—Book and Job.

Davis & Pitman, 137 Thames
Marshall & Flynn, 124 Thames
Sanborn J. P., 188 Thames
Ward Remington, Odd Fellows building, Washington square

Provision Dealers.

Bateman Benjamin, 5 and 7 Pelham
Barber Charles P., 4 and 6 Market square
Bryer Peleg, 21 and 23 Broadway
Burkinshaw & Marvel, 278 and 280 Thames
Carry Brothers, 187 and 189 Thames
Clark Thomas C., 32 Washington square
Crosby John H. Jr., Bellevue ave., cor. Levin
DeBlois John B., 15 Broadway
Dennis William E., 93 Thames
Denniston George, 26 Kinsley's wharf
Dodge William R. (market gardener), Warner,
 opposite Newport avenue
Greason Lawrence M., 308 Thames
Hazard George M., 2 Broadway
Lawton W. H. H., 13 Long wharf
Lee Brothers, 179 Thames
Pittman John, 19 Thames, corner Bridge
Potter Stephen A., 42 Broadway
Scott H. D., 223 Thames
Sherman C. & Co., 8 and 10 Market square
Spooner Edwin G., 54 Broadway
Stoddard William A., 90 Broadway
Sullivan Timothy W., 326 Thames
Tilley Abram A., 110 Broadway
Wallace Edward S., 20 Broadway
Williams Charles S., 28 Broadway

Real Estate Agents.

Crocker Edward A., Bellevue ave., cor. Kay
Ford Thomas G., Fludder's block, Bellevue av-
 enue, corner Catherine
Howard J. Neilson & Co., Bellevue avenue, n.
 Casino
PORTER FRANK B. & CO., Bellevue avenue,
 near Kay (see p. 24)
Smith Alfred & Sons, Bellevue ave., n. Mill
Watson Daniel, 165 Thames
Wilbur George V., Bellevue avenue, near Kay

Roofers and Roofing Materials.

Bowen George W. (rubber), over 23 Long wharf
Walsh Brothers (tin), 11 Market square

Sail and Awning Makers.

Cole Thomas, Perry Mill wharf
Hogan & Scott, 10 Commercial wharf
Matteson James M., 22 Washington square
Wilmarth George H., 22 Travers block, Belle-
 vue avenue

Sewing Machine Dealers.

Banning Carlos, 12 Broadway
Pritchard George A (Singer), Broadway, corner
 Marlborough
SHERMAN WALTER, (domestic and house-
 hold), 140 Thames (see p. 16)
Ward A. J., (Davis), Odd Fellows building,
 Washington square
WHEELER & WILSON MFG. CO., S H. Ken-
 ney manager, 86 Broadway (see p. 38)
Williams Charles S., 28 Broadway.

Skating Rink.

Olympian Club Roller Skating Rink, Bellevue
 avenue, near Ocean House.

Stables.

Barker William A. & Co., 13 Second.
Bowler William T., 3½ Brinley, near Kay
Carr Benjamin M., Howard near Spring
Casttoff Henry M., 18 Touro, corner Spring
Colvin James, State, near Clarendon court
Dawley Benj. H., State, near Clarendon court
Hayward E. & A. H., Downing, near Bellevue
 avenue
LAWTON GEORGE P., (livery sale and board-
 ing), 23 to 33 Marlboro (see insert opp. p. 63)
Murray Hiram, State, corner Clarendon court.
Rowley John H., Long wharf, near Thames
Smith J. L., Fillmore
Stewart A. & Son, 4 and 11 Pelham
Tennant, William C. Jr., 10½ Barney

Stove Dealers and Tinsmiths.

Brown James B., agent, 122 Thames
Covell W. K. Jr., 95 and 97 Thames
Goddard & Barlow, rear 122 Thames
Langley & Sharpe, 195 Thames
Marden James F., 4 and 5 Cottrell's block, 222
 Thames
Southwick J. M. K., 117 Thames
Walsh Brothers, 11 Market square

Stucco Workers.

Fludder W. & Co., Bellevue ave., c. Catherine
Underwood W. J., Weaver ave., n. Freebody

Submarine Engineer, Wrecker, and Diver.

Waters John, store, Commercial wharf, post-
 office box 47

Telegraph Companies.

Western Union Telegraph Co., Thomas J.
 Smith, manager, Thames, near Franklin,
 branch offices at Ocean and Perry Houses

Telephone Exchange.

NEWPORT AND SUBURBAN TELEPHONE
 EXCHANGE, 3d floor Gas Co.'s building, 177½
 Thames (see p. 36)

Toy Dealers.

LANDERS A. C., 165 Thames (see p. 30)
LUTHER A. W., Daily News block, 205 Thames
 (see p. 10)

Transportation Lines and Agents.

Continental Steamboat Co., J. S. Bliss, agent,
 Commercial wharf
Denniston Geo., agent for the Inman, Cunard,
 Williams & Guion, Hamburg, and Allan lines
 of steamers, 26 Kinsley's wharf
Newport and Wickford Railroad and Steam-
 boat Co., Theodore Warren, agent, Commer-
 cial wharf
Old Colony Steamboat Co., J. H. Jordan, agent,
 Long wharf

Trunks, Valises, Etc.

BIESEL HENRY, 176 Thames (see p. 14)
Gratrix George, 18 Broadway, and 10 Travers
 block Bellevue avenue
McCARTY BROS., Cottrell block, Thames (see
 insert, opp. p. 62)

Undertakers.

Bryer Stafford, 90 Thames
Cottrell M., 2 and 3 Cottrell's block, 222 Thames
Langley John S., 10 Franklin
McCormick Michael, Dearborn, near Spring
Shea John F., 142 Spring, corner Bowery

Veterinary Surgeons.

Heard J. M., 10 Travers block, Bellevue ave.
Hull George E. (eclectic), 4 Elm
Lineham George N., 17, 19 and 21 W. Broadway

Wheelwrights.

Cripps William W. L., Sherman, near Spring
Easterbrooks Benjamin T., Burnside court, n.
 Davis court
Holm, A. M., rear Long wharf
Scott Brothers, Spring, cor. Sherman
Seatle Charles H., Weaver ave., n. Freebody
Wood Andrew T., 6 Sherman

Columbia Bicycles and Tricycles.

To turn and ride a new Pegasus.
And witch the world with noble wheelmanship.

Go forth upon your wheeléd horse, and list
To Nature's teachings.

"Thou hast no faults, or I no faults can spy.
"Thou art all beauty, or all blindness I."

The Expert Columbia.
A medium-weight bicycle. The most artistic and scientific bicycle made.

The Columbia Standard Bicycle.
The "Old Reliable Steed" for general road use.

The Columbia Racer.
Some fourteen pounds lighter than the Expert. The most practical racer constructed.

The Columbia Tricycle.
For general use by ladies and gentlemen.

THE POPE MANUFACTURING COMPANY,
597 Washington St., Boston, Mass.
Send 3c. stamp for new Illustrated Catalogue, with price-list and full information.

The exercise of riding does not strain;
One moves as lightly as the rain from heaven,
Upon the wheeléd steed.

And now I see with eye serene,
The very pulse of the machine;
A being breathing thoughtful breath.
A lady getting life and health.

"Now good digestion wait on appetite,
"And health on both."

www.ingramcontent.com/pod-product-compliance
Lightning Source LLC
Chambersburg PA
CBHW021425090426
42742CB00009B/1252